SHOTO'S
TRADITIONAL KARATE KAI

SHOTO'S
TRADITIONAL KARATE KAI
MY LIFE, MY ART, IN KARATE AND TAI-CHI

Gerald Griffiths

authorHOUSE®

AuthorHouse™
1663 Liberty Drive
Bloomington, IN 47403
www.authorhouse.com
Phone: 1-800-839-8640

Published by AuthorHouse   12/07/2012

ISBN: 978-1-4772-4725-9 (sc)
ISBN: 978-1-4772-4726-6 (e)

THE SHOTO'S TRADITIONAL KARATE KAI

 In this book I wanted to pass on my experence and Standards of exellence, which I have carried over from my years of service I spent in the Grenadier Guards, and of the teaching standards of N.V.Q.'s in Combat sports within the Martial Arts. The communication and the teaching abilities, on how to get the best possible standard of technique, and practices of your students. To pass on the research of diet and of my own standard of fitness and advice on the ability that I have achieved throughout my life.

Within the book you will be able to see that with out the help of some of my instructors, The late Sensei Viv Nash being one of those instructors, whom I admire and have the utmost respect for, I would never have been able to achieve so much. R.I.P.

Also the enjoyment of training with the late Sensei Les Mclean whom I also have the utmost respect for, and Looking back on the fun and humour and the excellence of training he brought on the mat, within the Martial Art of Aki-Do, and Ju-Jitsu. R.I.P.

I also hope that you will enjoyed my book, and I have been able to give you a good insight to our Tai-Chi and Karate, as well as the hints on well being, diet and fittness.

SHOTO'S
TRADITIONAL KARATE KAI

MY LIFE MY ART IN KARATE AND TAI-CHI.

THE LIFE OF AN X-GRENADIER GUARDSMAN
&
MARTIAL ARTIST,
HIS LIFE EXPERIENCE,
AND THE FUNDAMENTAL EXCELLENCE
OF TEACHING TO THE STANDARDS OF N.V.Q.'S.

GERALD GLYN GRIFFITHS.

THE AUTHOR, THE MAN THE MASTER, IN TAI-CHI AND KARATE.

The life's experience of an X-Grenadier Guardsman.
A Martial Arts Instructor and Sensei
of
Shoto's Traditional Karate Kai

His Life's expeience and the fundamental standard of
excellience
for
teaching to the standards of N.V.Q.'s,
in the art of Karate & Tai-Chi and the fitness
of which you would like to achieve

THE FRONT COVER SAYS IT ALL.

WHICH INCIDENTALLY IS THE AUTHOR?

he would like to pass on his research of Diet
and of
his own experience's of fitness
and
advice on the ability to achieve the quality he has had.

At the age of over sixty nine
he is still going strong
and
manages to keep on keeping on.
living his life to the full.

Some
Photographic
Artistic Pictures
you may like to see.

Kwanku Dai.

9

SHOTO BARI.

SIDE KICK.

The complete Graphic design and typing
Of all the
Pages were done by Gerald Glyn Griffiths.

The complete Graphic design and typing
Of all the
Pages were done by Gerald Glyn Griffiths.

Dedications & Thanks.

Chapter (1)

Dedications & Thanks.

I would like to dedicate this book with love, to my Son, Graham John Griffiths. My Grandson, Brandon John Griffiths, My Granddaughter, Larrisa Fay Griffiths.

I would like to dedicate this book, to all Soldiers that has died in the world doing their duty for their countryman, in order so we may live in a safe democratically free society, without dictatorship and fear, and to all my family and Friends.

Dedications go to my most important teachers that have taught me so much.

The late Sensei Viv Nash and the late Sensei Les Maclean.

Also thanks to Sensei Mitsuzuki Harada, my first teacher and Sensei. Also thanks to all Sensei's that has contributed to the improvements of my Martial Arts.

I would like to thank all my students, past and present, for their dedication in training and giving me their time and for their permission and help with photos in the book.

Sensei Robert Huntley, 5th Dan. My second in command, he is now the Sensei for Great Britain. Bob and I have also been on national T.V. showing our art, and as partners in Martial Arts, we are a force that can show the abilities of practice and practice.

Bob has shown me dedication and loyalty over the last thirty years, he has the ability to work hard and maintain a standard of fitness up and beyond the normal capacity of the average person. Bob's outstanding attention to detail and perfection shows in his work. He is a quiet man, with a strong outward energy force, which presents confidence to the atmosphere of the Do-Jo. This confidence brings security in everything he does, I am proud to be his teacher and friend.

He is a good ambassador for the martial arts, and a great instructor for Britain.

And to all, up and coming students within our groups, may they all carry on meliorating and becoming good Karate-ka within their own right, to be good people?

Steven Walker, Ian Parry, Tony Williams, Alex Bowen, Lesley Cook, Kirstie Cratchley, James Merritt, Brian Morse, Kevin Ellis, James Macintyre, Mark and Rob Cook.

Some kind words
By
Sensei Robert Huntley 5th Dan.

Some kind words
By
Sensei Robert Huntley 5th Dan.

I have known Gerald Griffiths for over 30 years. In that time he has become a close friend within the Martial Arts and outside. He is a man who shows interest in others and I feel that I have become part of his family.

Practicing for over forty years; Martial Arts have become his life. He shows complete dedication and understanding. His teaching qualities make him extremely valuable to the Martial Arts World, as he gives so much of his time to passing on his knowledge and experience to others.

R. B. Huntley .... Colleague

13

'Such a parting should have made a greater crack'
Anthony and Cleopatra Shakespeare

Sifu Griff,

I well remember the first time I visited your dojo. Over the years I had
trained with two tai chi teachers. The first taught me the Yang short form
and it seemed to be mainly an exercise in memory and quiet relaxation. The
second taught me the long form which took two years! He was seeking the
elusive, mystical chi energy and seemed obsessed with the tiniest detail of
each move which he thought would enhance this magic. I was not convinced
and my skepticism grew when I discovered that he became angry and
possibly intimidated when I voiced my many questions. It began feeling like
a cult. With a Karate background in my teens I was very interested in the
martial applications but his answers seemed fatuous to me. So I read every
book I could get hold of but I longed for a teacher who could show me.

There is a Buddhist proverb that when the desire becomes strong, the teacher
will arrive. So I remember that night by the canal. Your other students had
not come so there was just the two of us. You demonstrated the form that I
knew so well but it was transformed. For every one of my simple postures
you seemed to incorporate a number of intricate maneuvers and when I
asked you what they meant and you demonstrated on me I felt you were
always just out of reach and I was always precariously off balance. What is
more you welcomed my questions! I had found my teacher!

All that was several years ago now but every time we have met I have
learned something new: from the 'double tap' to the whirlwind waltz of
endless relaxed engagement. I have admired your years of dedicated
training, your endless willingness to learn, your 'no nonsense' pragmatism
and your ingenuity in discovering fresh applications.

So Griff, it is an understatement to say that I will miss you and I am not sure
where I will go from here but both Susan and I wish you and June a
wonderful future in Oz. You have made an indelible impact on me and I
leave you with my blessing.

CONTENT
OF
SHOTO'S TRADITIONAL KARATE KAI

Chapters (1) to (31)

Chapter (2)

Authors Preface & Introduction

Shoto`s traditional-Karate-Kai

Karate & Tai-Chi.

Within the nucleus of Shoto's Traditional Karate-Kai, we have put together workouts with effective precision moves combined from both arts, Karate & Tai-Chi.

Looking to target and focusing on arms, thighs, hips & abs. In addition, with focusing on the Chi-Kung breathing, which will increase your heart rate and breathe of the lungs & circulation?

We work to traditional warm ups and Kihon, Kata, and Sampon Kimute, but with the same body condition as the soft form of Tai-Chi. So by integrating our Tai-Chi with Karate with no conflict with the other, our moves are that much more flowing, with a strong concentration, focusing on Chi, (the intrinsic energy) that's within us all.

You have to inhale the new air of your breathing, going from the soft and hard, to hard and soft with your movements. To cultivate this, you concentrate on *(Tu-Na)* exhalation (Old air),

The best form to find this is the Chen form. Within the Chen form, you can see the soft hard movements of Karate, and the softness of Tai-Chi.

The Chen Form synchronizes the inner outer harmonies 'The Ying & Yang', tranquilising, and harmonizing into one. This is not physical strength. Physical strength prevents the flow of Chi, (the intrinsic energy) through the body.

As you move through the forms, whether they are Kata or Tai-Chi, relax with concentrated breathe.

Then your harmonized movements become tranquil and relaxed, the life fluid Chi, can then be more circulated by the motion of exercise.

With the breath from your lower *(tan Tain)*, Lower Psychic Centre, this energy is sustained with the rhythm. The top half of the body is made soft and light *(Yin)*. The lower half is lowered and made heavy (Yan) as possible, but both halves are still in perfect coordination with each other.

Stretching your movements from front stance, to back stance, in an unbroken sequence and the spine is rotating within these movements. Making your movements as graceful as possible, with their mechanics and your concentrated breath, they will become therapeutic to improve your health, preserve, and rehabilitate your potential for a longer life.

The exercises for Tai-Chi are complementary therapeutic for the elderly and people who suffer the aging problems of Rheumatoid Arthritis, Osteoarthritis!

They can be done with vigour and a daily exercise for lifelong physical fitness, which will slow down the degenerative aging process and promote physical psychological health reducing stress and depression and anxiety.

As an Instructor and Non Commissioned Officer in the Grenadier Guards, has taught me a lot on how to supervise and get the best out of a class of men. During and after the forces I have been practising Combat Arts with a considerable amount of dedication. With all this in mind, I have put these writings down with the intention of passing on the knowledge I have gained on instruction, communication and relationships with others, and of course karate information on what is taught in 'Shoto's Traditional Karate Kai'.

I do sincerely hope you will look and study this book, rather than just glance through it. Remember I have tried to help explain techniques, not just on combat arts, but also on instruction, demonstration and communication.

A practitioner of combat arts must train his mind as well as his body; therefore! I have put thoughts and philosophy of great men in my writing.

Paul Collins, kicking a side kick, against Steven Owen.

My first approach to Karate.

In my army training I was more aggressive and my combat was of quite a different nature 'very military' and aggressive. This was fine for army life, for this was not so much an art but part of my army survival and training,

Because of this during my early years as a serious martial artist I found it very hard to relax, I only thought of the fighting aspect of Karate, 'I found it hard to be myself'.

At first in Karate, I learned I was testing myself, and it was difficult to understand what I was practising for.

I found many of the tests were of my own making and not of my instructors.

'Because I was thinking of fighting all the time my instructors gave me a hard time'. In addition, I was quite aggressive in my attitude to practice.

Looking back with hindsight into 'The Karate-Do-Shotokai', I realise many hardships and test were of my own making, 'within me', and my own imagination, also my actions were illustrious, and I made efforts to imbricate others.

I now know that the tests from my instructors were of my own and not there's. After a few years of practice, I began to correct my aberrant ways and concentrated on improving the equanimity of my mind.

Patience is built up through the years! You need control to avoid losing your temper with difficult students and rough opponents. This is why it is inviolable you have strict discipline and Do-Jo etiquette.

This will help to produce better people to become inter-dependent on each other, which can build equanimity in their lives?

The rigid hierarchical structures within the Do-Jo can emphasise the student to try to achieve much more, to move higher in this hierarchical structure, thus! Setting standards for ourselves as instructors and students alike.

I personally have found, as I got older and have still been able to practice hard, setting an example.

Therefore it spreads not only with young students, but with some of my most senior instructors. 'By setting a precedent in this way', I hope with modesty, my and their attitude towards practice strengthens. In addition! I hope the human spiritual qualities I have given my most senior students are pasted on to the beginner student. Because of this, I have been able to bring together friendship and loyalty within my own club. Although a small club compared to those in the cities it is a strong club.

'I will still carry on trying to reach more goals and continue to progress my own practice'.

Sensei Griffiths Smashing Ten Tiles.

Chapter (3)

SHOTO'S TRADITIONAL
KARATE – KAI
CHIEF INSTRUCTOR
GERALD G GRIFFITHS

| United Kingdom. | Wales. | Gloucester. | United-states. | Australia. |

The flags signify the place's in which our martial arts has a lot of connections in our teaching.

Sensei Gerald Griffiths: A flying kick at Stinchcombe hill.

Sensei Gerald Griffiths' profile.

I have practised Martial Arts for over 40 years, consisting of Karate, Tai-Chi, Bo-Staff, Broadsword, Boken, Knife Self Defence and Chi Kung Breathing.

Our style of Karate consists of rhythmic continuous movements, on practising Kata very much like Tai Chi, so that our Karate and Tai Chi go hand in hand.

I have practised and trained with some of the best Instructors and Sensei in the World, including such names as, Sensei's Vivian Nash, Les Maclean, Mitsuzuki Harada, Toru Takamizawa, Wayne Scott, John Richards, and Eugene Godrington, Edd Cook, Edd Naumowicz, Tom Hudako, Grandville Steel and Brian (Skippy) Whipps, Billy Griffiths and Kevin O'Connor.

Mitsusuki Harada and Toru Takamizawa, both Japanese instructors, with a very strict discipline and teaching method.

My first instructor and Sensei was Mitsuzuki Harada.

1971   Shoto-Kai under Mitsuzuki Harada 5th Dan.
        Trained every summer camp from 1973-80.

1980   Tera-Karate-Kai under Toru Takamizawa.
        Retook coloured belts 3rd kyu 11-07-80, 2nd kyu 16-11-80.

1981   Shoto-Ryu Karate under Viv Nash 7th Dan.
        Tai-Chi within Shoto-Ryu.

1983   Awarded 1st Dan (Shoto-Ryu Karate)

1984   Awarded 2nd Dan (Shoto-Ryu Karate)

1987   Awarded 3rd Dan (Shoto-Ryu Karate)

1982-87 Trained at all Summer Schools.

1992   Founded Shoto's Traditional Karate-Kai, as Chief Instructor, under the umbrella of Shikon

1993   Awarded 4th Dan. 1999
Became a Bushi Karate-Jitsu Regional Director. Awarded 5th Dan.

Trained in the Armed and Combat Forces since 1961, till 1973, and Karate since 1971 and Tai-Chi since 1981.

Clubs held:

Club Instructor, South Gloucestershire Karate Club Wotton-under-Edge – 10 years.

Club Instructor, Sharpness Karate Club Sharpness – 1 year. Club Instructor, Quedgeley Karate Club Gloucester – 1978 until 2010 Chief Instructor for Shoto Traditional Karate-Kai Great Britain – 1992 to 2010 I then emigrated to Australia, handing the club and the British Shoto's group to Sensei Robert Huntley.

Regional Director, Bushi Karate Jitsu Association – 1998 to 2009.
On 12th March 2010 was awarded my 6th Dan with the ButoKukai Fellowship Trust Awarded by Sensei Whipps 7th Dan and Sensei B Griffiths 6th Dan and Sensei S cook 6th Dan.

Chapter (4)

Miyamoto Musashi.

A very famous formidable Warrior of his time was Miyamoto Musashi, born in 1584! He was a most renowned warrior. A Samurai devoted to the art of Japanese Sword Fencing! 'kendo'.

He had won so many contests of swordsmanship, and of about sixty contests killed all his opponents.

Because of his formidable ability, he decided to write a book to formulate his philosophy, called Go Rin No Sho, translated in English is named, 'The Book of Five Rings'. He had finished writing it in a Mountain in Kyushu. And a few weeks later before his death in 1645, such a short life of only 56 years old he had become a legend in Japan.

This book was not only on philosophy, but on strategy and cunning. From this lots of businessmen run their businesses on his strategy running sales like operations like a military company. 'Influenced by the Zen philosophy', 'Shinto' and the Confucianism behind and outside of kendo. He was to most readers as coming over as a very cruel and merciless man.

Sometime through the book, I found it so hard to understand the ideal of his strategy at first but if you keep reading over and over studying his ethos you can be enlightened by his extraordinary path of Martial Strategy. With Businessman this path of Miyamoto's strategy became part of the treachery in trades and industry throughout Japan. 'The Book of Five Rings' became almost like a Bible in the world of industrial espionage. Also in Politics, Political prominent people and anyone who could use his strategy to further their own businesses and industrial supermarkets would keep his book on their desk.

It is now much more formidable to succeed with these strategies now, what with computers and modern technology, receiving experienced commensurate amount of materials against your business's opponents.

I have read his book so many times and as a martial artist I have tried so hard to live my life as a good person rather than as a bad person and you can still use his strategies for the good to make friend and for people to like you.

Sensei Mitsusuki Harada was very kind to have autographed my book of five Rings which you can see

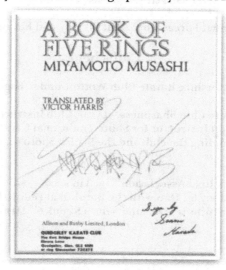

here.

12th — 13th Century
JAPANESE COMMANDER
(TAISHO)

Drawn by Alan Nash

Japanese Samurai warrior.

Commissioned & Drawn and painted by 'Alan Nash' of which I have the original.

Chapter (5)   # History of karate.

KARATE: the art of Empty-Hand Fighting is an excellent means of Self-Defence, which relies on the effective use of the unarmed body. Through systematic training of the techniques of blocking or thwarting an attack and counter-attacking the opponent by punching, striking, kicking, the human body can become as effective as an actual weapon.

So throughout history, in the distant past, the origins of karate began with the ability to defend oneself. In Asia and the Middle East there were a lack of Police Forces and law and order unlike we have today. People created a variety of Martial Arts, which allowed them to defend themselves effectively.

To understand the historical development of the present day Karate, we must go back to the ancient Chinese art of Kempo (*Chuan-Fa*). The roots of Chuan-Fa can be found in a group of physical exercises, which intended to allow people to live to a great age.

In the later period animal movements were adopted to these exercises, and it began to develop into a form of hand to hand fighting.

In the Far East and China, a Shaolin Monk, 'Daruma Bodhidharma', as he was known in Japanese, developed Martial Art Schools, There was a lot of trading between China and Japan on and around the Islands of Okinawa. With the blend of these two countries, the Martial Arts evolved, this then became Okinawa-te, the Te meaning Hand, Kara that means Empty, as in a void, became Kara-Te.

According to legend, in the year 517 A.D. the Indian Zen Master, Bodhidharma *(Daruma)* travelled to China and taught Buddhism to Chinese Monks at a Monastery called Shaolin-Sze. Because of the poor physical condition of the Student Monks, he instituted a system of physical and mental discipline embodied in the I-Chin Sutra. Soon the Monks at Shaolin-Sze became known as the best fighters in China.

Over many years, these systems of unarmed combat intermingled and eventually developed into the art of Chuan-Fa (Kempo).

Okinawa, which is the main island of the Ryukyu Chain, was in contact with both China and Japan and probably *(Chan-fa)* Kempo was imported along with many other elements of Chinese Culture. *(Chuan-fa)* Kempo may very probably have been combined with some native form of hand-to-hand fighting to produce Okinawa-Te.

It is that later, during the rule of Okinawa by King Hashi and afterwards the Satsuma Clan, all weapons was seized and possession of them strictly forbidden.

As a result of these bans against weapons, the art of empty-hand self-defence underwent tremendous development.

Peasants practiced Karate because the rulers would not allow ordinary people to carry weapons and the arts remained secret.

It was in the 1900's that Okinawa-Te came to the fore with a public demonstration and in 1901 was then taught as a sport in schools on Okinawa.

Master FUNAKOSHI Gichin

富名腰　義珍
Fu　Na　Koshi　　Gi　Chin

The man most responsible for the introduction of modern-day Karate to Japan was Gichin Funakoshi. Born in Okinawa, where he studied under the top masters, he was the first man to introduce Karate to Japan proper in 1917.

Funakosh was born in Okinawa in 1868. In 1922 Funakoshi was invited by the Emperor of Japan to do a demonstration in Tokyo and this was a great success.

Funakoshi's fame then spread and during the year 1936 his Do-jo, (Studio, Gymnasium) was founded in Tokyo.

In 1922 Gichin Funakoshi a professor from Okinawa, regarded now as the founder of modern karate, was invited to mainland Japan.

He was asked to demonstrate Okinawa-Te or Kara-Te as a part of presentation of ancient Japanese Martial Arts, his demonstration made such a lasting impression on those who saw it, that Funakoshi was asked to stay in Japan and teach Karate.

He taught at various Universities before he founded the style of Karate, which we know today as Shotokan, Shotokan comprises of two words. In Japanese Shoto was the pen name of Funakoshi, and Kan meaning Hall, area or meeting place.

After the Karate-Do of Sensei Funakoshi spread to most Universities throughout Japan, the founder of Ju-Do, Jigaro Kano asked Funakoshi to lecture about his Karate at the Kodokan, (Gym or Judo Hall) and this was a very big turning point for Funakoshi, so he stayed on in Tokyo to completely teach and promote his Karate.

Some of the best Karate experts came through from this era! Shigeru Egami, Hironishi, and one of the most important was his own son, Yoshitaka Funakoshi, he was based at the Waseda University.

Karate quickly became an integral part of Japanese Culture. From there, thanks to the foresight of the various masters, Karate began to spread throughout the World.

It came slowly at first and then as the hitherto veil of secrecy lifted from the deadly fighting art, interest escalated at an amazing rate. It's phenomenal impact upon Europe was first felt in France and from there spread like wildfire, until practically every country now has its own National Karate Teams.

Photo by Richard Olpin.

Sensei Griffiths.

Other's who Followed in Gichin Funakoshi's footsteps were great Masters from Okinawa, who in turn introduced other varying forms of the art? Consequently, these developed not one, but many styles of Karate, some demanding great power to execute, some depending upon blinding speed and super agility, others blending all these qualities to varying degrees, depending on the views of the particular Masters of that style.

But in 1957 Master Funakoshi died so the Waseda group established the Shotokai which means Shoto's Council. Sensei Gerald Griffiths, the author, and the Chief Instructor for Shotos Traditional Karate Kai, kept this (Shoto's) title because of his direct link to teachers he practiced Karate with, under the direction of Sensei Mitsuzuki Harada of the Karate-do-Shotokai.

Sensei Mitsuzuke Harada received his 5th Dan directly from Sensei Gichin Funakoshi.

Book photo, back cover.

Sensei Shihan Gerald Griffiths, ESQ.

With a Sidekick to his opponent.

Taken at Wayne Scott's Club, in Australia.

Gerald also practised with Sensei Viv Nash's,

Shoto Ryu Karate Kai for a considerable time.

The late Sensei Viv Nash was also a student of Mitsuzuki Harada.

Gerald has the greatest of respect for Sensei Viv Nash, of his teaching, and the enjoyment of years practicing under him, which contributed to his ability in Karate. In Shoto Kai and Shoto Ryu, Competition Karate was never practised and it is the same with Shoto's Traditional Karate Kai.

Gerald believes as do Sensei Viv Nash, that Kata, Sampon, Kumite and sparring within the club is enough for a student to become mellow improve and demonstrate their mastery of technique.

Our Grading Syllabus is very extensive. All our Karate, Kata, and body condition are very much the same as Tai Chi. Our Kata flow on smooth continuous movements, with a very low stance; this will help a student find his centre.

There is no conflict between our Tai Chi and Karate, as our posture and movements are rounded and circular. We practise Sticky Hand, Push Hand, the Long Yang and Chen Style Tai Chi, all these practices improves our Karate.

The Chi Kung breathing and the way you breathe is the same way we breathe in Tai Chi and Karate. This gives a far better understanding of sensitivity, which in turn gives us a better flow of energy (Chi), we also use weapons to help extend and project our (Ki) Chi Energy.

Chapter (6)

Mitsusuke Harada.

I took up karate as a serious Martial Artist with Sensei Mitsusuki Harada.

He was another of Sensei Funakoshi's student's, Sensei Mitsusuki Harada, born 16th November 1928 in Dairen on the Southern tip of Manson Yuteke. Sensei Harada joined the Shotokai Dojo in 1943.

The Master's of those days were Master Hironishi Genshin, Wada Uemura and Yashiaki Hayasha.

Sensei Mitsusuki Harada was trained by Hiroishi Genshin. But had trained with Funakoshi and Yoshitaka, and later around 1948 trained with Kamata Toshio, Egami Shigera and Okuyama Tadao.

Harada being one of the few men still living today, who trained under Funakoshi's family.

He introduced Karate as we know it today to Brazil in 1955, the same year he received his 5th Dan, (Godan) at the age of 28 directly from Master Funakoshi. Out of respect for Funakoshi he took his Dan Grades no further.

Then travelling to Europe in 1963 and also teaching in France at the invitation of Henri Plee.

All though I only took up Martial Arts seriously in 1973, I like to think that the years service spent in the Armed Forces, as in armed and unarmed combat, contributed to the long years of experience for my Martial Arts, after all that is what it is. 'Military Art'.

In 1973 I started with Shoto-Kai under Mitsazuke Harada 5th Dan where I achieved first Kyu by 1975. It was with hard-dedicated training in addition to attending all of the Summer Schools during this time.

On the left,

my record of grade's from Sensei Harada

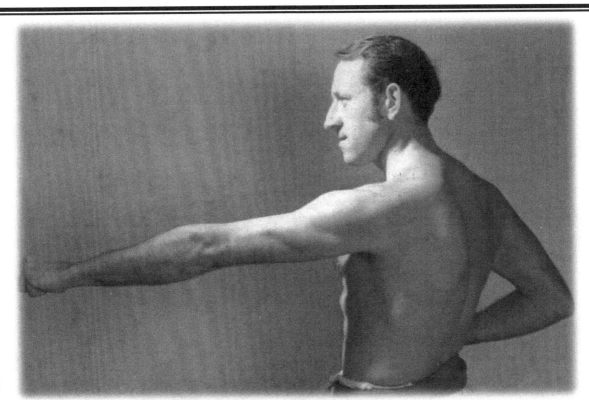

Sensei Griffiths, as a young Green Belt, aged 33 years old. 1974.

'Wish I was still 33'.

Gerald sparring with Dean George at his gym, at the Rea Bridge House.

Sensei Harada Blocking with the Bo, from an attack of Oi zuke, by Mike Peacock.

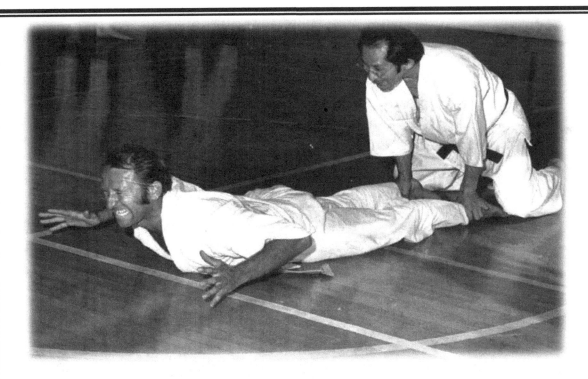

Sensei Harada demonstrating pressure points.

Sensei Griffiths, blocking with Shoto-Bari, from an Oi zuke from Sensei Mitsusuki Harada. 1976.

Sensei Harada, demonstrating defence from an attack by Mike Peacock, at the South Gloucestershire Karate Club 1976. Sensei Griffiths kneeling down nearest camera.

Black and Brown Belt course, about 1979.

Sensei Mitusuzki Harada on the left, on the right with beard Sensei Gerald Griffiths.

Sensei Mitsusuki Harada, helping and demonstrating to a student how to defend against an attack of Oi Zuki Jodan from Sensei Gerald Griffiths.

Summer Schools with Shotokai in the Old school were so hard.

To survive Summer School and to give off one's best 'with honour!' with Sensei Harada let alone doing eight of them on consecutive years. To survive one was a feet in its self, 'Let alone eight'. They consisted of five days of intense training, ten to twelve hours a day, pushing ourselves beyond our limits. I remember the first day my feet were bleeding and red-raw and still having to grit my teeth and practice, and still with four days to go. With this you had to draw on all yourselves, inner power of energy and Strength. I attended Summer Schools consecutively from 1974 through to 1979.

In the beginning training under Sensei Harada was great and for a few years, with my enthusiasm I felt that my training in Shotokai was going from strength to strength. After demob from the Grenadier Guards, I felt this was something I could really get my teeth into. I knew I would carry on doing Martial Arts for the rest of my life.

2nd 3rd /February/1974 was one of our clubs first courses with the Shotokai; Sensei Jimmy Woods was the Black Belt that came to us. He was amazing with his strength of fitness, and this was something I enjoyed so much, the physical within my Martial Arts was always something I wanted to improve on and enjoy. So when Jimmy Woods introduced us to the Demon Bunny hops, which he showed with amazing strength and power, I was impressed. To tell you about this power of Bunny Hops I will leave it to Mr Ivor-ward-Davies. He was a reporter that trained at our club in those early years. Quote:

AH SO! IT'S THE BUNNY SECRETS OF KUNG FU:

BY IVOR-WARD-DAVIES

After a study of one particular form of the magic sport of today, Martial Arts, the secret of defeating any devotee of these Oriental Fighting Forms can be revealed.

Look your belated adversary straight in the eyes and order him to 'BUNNY HOP'. This simple phrase will transform him from a demon into a wincing human, his eyes glaze, he sinks down to a squat and hops meekly away.

Most outsiders to these weird forms of fighting imagine that students of the sports learn how to shatter bricks, pieces of wood, sculls, various bones and bullies' egos with frightening ease.

Well, as a beginner to Karate, I can refute every one of those ideas from the bottom of each aching muscle, which is all of them:

Choosing Karate was easy. The club was closest to home and I was adding a few inches to what used to be a lithe-some form', with trouser-splitting results. Karate appealed to my nature, and being comparatively small in stature, I wanted to defend myself.

Also in this style of Karate the blows are never 'SUPPOSED' to land, so no damaged eyes, throat, legs, toes, or anything that lies in between.

LESSON ONE.

Answering an advert in a paper, I joined forty other beginners in various stages of undress in a school gymnasium. Age did not matter, nor size, eager students ranged from under twelve to thirty.

After a few limbering exercises the secret method of defeat was revealed, smile sweetly and say in a stern voice- 'BUNNY HOPPINGBEGIN'.

How many times we bunny hopped around that room I cannot say, but we all finished doing something like a worm crawl'. After dozens of laps we were told to stand up, half of us immediately fell over again. Our knees were refusing to lock in the erect position. Great I thought 'no need to fight any one, I can jump over them and bunny hop into the sunset'. I spent hours in a radox bath, rubbing rheumatic ointments into my swollen muscles and keeping as still as possible. Finally, I was felling reasonable aging, so I took lesson two. More bunny hopping, I began to wonder whether I had joined a rabbit's appreciation class. Then more limbering exercises. Whether those instructors had shares in the National Trust Organization I do not know, but every aching exercise we were told to move slowly from the set position or you will get a rupture.

It is amazing how slowly people can move with that threat hanging over there,,,,,,,,,,, heads.

By lesson three, we were practicing some of the set movements, 'soon' I thought, 'I will be able to smash bricks, or anything or anybody else that comes within range of my killing digits'. Now you know why rabbits do not need to know Kung-Fu.

All that kept me hopping was the hope of being able to stop. Looking back at the lesson, I cannot remember anything else other than bunny hoping for hours. It gave me tonsillitis four days later, but in those four days, I was in the most agonizing state, I could not walk, bend my legs, sit down, stand up or even drive. From the waist down, I was one torrent of pain. After five minutes, I realized I was correct, now I could defend myself. But only if my opponent came from one direction doing exactly the same attack in slow motion, 'AH-HA' think I again. The Kung-Fu film of Cain is really slowed up when he attacks with devilish kicks;

'He is only moving at half a mile an hour'.

Then I saw the instructors doing it properly, at full speed, and the truth dawned. Karate is not easy; it takes years and years of practice, training and study. Which is what a sport that can teach a person to kill, should be, to teach the mind and the body? Complete muscle control.

So now I realized that I will not be breaking bricks in the near future. I enjoy the art as a sport, and will continue to practice. But not to be able to hammer seven people at a time without ruffling my hair

"Two students doing Bunny hops; Brother's Nick and Richard King".

'By 'Must Go, time for practice'.

EXIT ONE JOURNALIST BUNNY HOPPING

'Kind permission of the Dursley & Gloucestershire Gazette'.

White belt doing spectacular Mora Geri (double kick) from a Bunny Hop.

Book cover photo: This is a hill at Stinchcome, Nr Dursley, and Gloucester, England.

Sensei Griffiths, doing a Star Jump from the Bunny Hop position.

Flying kick, by Sensei Griffiths at the Rea Bridge house.

A flying kick, against an attack by Sensei Robert Huntley.

At RAF Quedgely Main Gate, with a Meteor Jet in the background.

At the end of 1974 beginning of 1975, I became the Club Instructor for the South Gloucestershire Karate Club and had quite a few courses with Sensei Harada including at our club and going away most weekends, to one end of the Country to the other,

Due to some misunderstanding, over whether I was left or right handed on a course in 1976 with Sensei Harada; Sensei Harada was quite put out by this misunderstanding, as he thought I was right handed, and had thought I had cheated when he attacked me, my attack was for him to demonstrate something. He told me to put my favoured attacking hand to the back of his neck. I am left hand so I put my left hand there , when he turned to block my hand at his neck, he left himself open to a counter attack.

This infuriated him and he became quite angry, and said, 'No, No! I said your right hand, I reminded him, 'he said my favoured hand', which is exactly what I used. No you are right handed he said, no Sensei I am a left hander, 'he thought I was lying to cover up my mistake'. He got me to attack him with my right hand then my left, trying to judge if I was left or right handed and throughout that day, it was very tough and hard, As the day drew on, because of the grief he was giving me.

I tried to reason with him by apologizing to him for the misunderstanding, he thought I was now climbing down and admitting I was right handed. He was very pleased as he must have thought he had lost face in front of the people on the course, and said to everyone, 'ha! Mr Griffiths has said sorry for what he had done, but in fact I had only said sorry for the misunderstanding, 'not that I was right handed or had put my wrong hand there'.

When the course finished, I had to sit with Sensei Harada to make out the Grading Forms. I had to sign some of his paperwork. When he handed me the pen he gave it to me in my right hand, of which I naturally put into my left hand to write.

When the secretary took him to the train station to go back home to London, he asked the club secretary, why Mr Griffiths wrote with his left hand after admitting he was right handed. I do know he, 'the secretary', did not stick up for me and told Sensei Harada that I was right handed; he did fail his grade, maybe that had something to do with it.

After this, on lots of courses and meetings with Sensei Harada several times at Summer School and other weekend courses, it was never put right. Even when Sensei Harada probably found out that (IN FACT I WAS LEFT HANDED), Word got around about it, and this then rubbed off on to most of the other senior executive Dan Grades in the Shotokai, and I was given a very hard time, when Senior Dan Grades attack me in practice it was always full on, 'Sometimes I did get hurt!' Being an Ex-Regular Forces guy, I was used to hard training and having a hard time, so what in fact, they did was, 'and did not realize', they made me stronger, and more determined to succeed as a good human being, and a good Karate-Ka. I would like to think that this lesson made me a better instructor and was able to induce humility into my teaching, and never become too big to admit to a mistake.

For four long years after, I endeavoured to please Sensei Harada with my dedication to keep on trying to give off my best in practice, but to no prevail even to the fact that Students that had started with me right from there beginning as a novice, which I had brought on to become good Karate Ka's my own Students were up graded higher than myself, One of my students, "Adrian Baker" was awarded his black belt on the Summer School that we attended, and as I was genuinely pleased for him; congratulated him on it.

A Senior Executive rang me up to say are you going on this Black Belt Grading Course in Scotland and over the phone he seemed to imply that I should go as it would be important to me. I thought that with this, 'they', "the Senior Executive's were mellowing towards me and that my hard work had, and was finally going to be recognised. I ended going on this course which was a long way and very expensive which I could not really afford. We trained on the Saturday and that night Awards were given out for Dan Grades. Some of the things said while giving out the awards, I felt was directed at me. And then they gave one of my students-Student, which came on this course his Dan Grade, I was so disappointed, so all my hard work for them, was never recognised.

During the awards, Sensei Viv Nash, who was a Senior Executive of Shotokai and I was having a drink, and he was standing with me when they announced the Students Award of the Dan Grade. He turned to me and said that it was not fair, the way I had been treated over the last few years.

Sensei Viv Nash was the only Senior Black Belt Executive who had ever shown me respect, and had sympathised with the way I was treated throughout the years training, that I did in Shotokai. He had always fought in my corner. I will tell you some more about that later.

The next day on the Sunday I still trained and showed what I was made of. I am sure some of the other Executives were very surprised that I had not gone trait home after the awards. I never ever felt this student responsible for any of this and was pleased for him on obtaining his black belt,

I Left the South Gloucestershire Karate Club as they had a Black Belt to teach them, because of this and because I had moved to a new address in Quedgeley, Gloucester.

I then started a new club where I now lived, I registered it with the affiliation to Shotokai with over thirty members so I was not turned down, I then dedicated my life to bringing this club on, which became bigger than the South Gloucestershire Karate Club and with really good Karate guy's that I had brought on from novices. Adrian Baker had taken over from me in South Gloucestershire Karate club. Incidentally he was made up as the Area Executive for South Gloucestershire, and he came to my club, now that it was a large group and successful. He told me and one of my students he has been instructed to take over my club on Shotokai's behalf. This is what he said and that he did not really want to do it, but that he was instructed to do this, he did not realise that my students where loyal to me. Obviously he was shown the door.

One of the following weekend courses in Cardiff, which I attended, before I left to attend this course I had written out my resignation to leave Shotokai. I thought I would train and at the end of the course I would hand it over, two of the Senior Executive, Ziggy Boban secretary and 'Steven Hope', from Southampton were talking with me before I done this, and said Harada Sensei is mellowing towards you and to keep my head down, you will be all right. Probably that they realized and knew they could not take my club from me. I thought, 'too little too late', as I had made up my mind to leave. I then handed in my notice, and left with my head held high! 'It was there loss.

Since then I and are club has had some amazing experiences, throughout its entire life, through to this very day, which I hope you will enjoy reading about.

Sensei Griffiths showing Ude-uke & Gedan-Bara. 20010.

This is a small group of some of the Quedgeley members on a club night around 1990

Sensei Griffiths doing a flying kick for the kids at Sensei Brian Morse's Club

Tony-Pandy in South/Wales. The young lad second from right James Merritt kneeling.

He became an outstanding Black Belt, and instructor of the club as you will see later in the book.

Chapter (7)   **Sensei Toru Takamizawa**

We as a club needed to belong to an official governing body, to survive and have insurance for our members, so in 1980 we started with the Tera-Karate-Kai under the late Sensei Toru Takamizawa I then retook all my Kyu Grades of coloured belts, from 3rd kyu to 1st kyu.

Sensei Griffiths with the Late Sensei Toru Takamizawa & Sensei Time Cale.

During that time, I and some of my students attended Summer School two consecutive years.

The training was hard, that was the way I liked it. For that was how I trained all the time. Robert Huntley and I would always go for the burn in all we do.

Both being Ex Forces and all.

Which was the only way, we knew how to train.

One of Sensei Takamizawa's students was Eugenue Godrington. Eugeneu Codrington was a very prominent figure when I was practicing with Sensei Toru Takamizawa. He had a nick name called the Cat. He was awarded his 7th Dan in Karate in June 1998; he started training when just 17 years old, and with very intensive training, was graded with his 1st Dan, less than two and a half years later.

Training at the Temple Karate Centre in Birmingham which was where his Instructor Sensei Toru Takamizawa instructed, which is where I first met Sensei Toru and also training on the Summer Camps with him.

The Quedgeley Karate Club students receiving their Student of the Year Awards 1980.

Chapter (8)

Sensei Viv Nash.

Sensei Viv Nash was born in 1931, at Radstock near Bristol, in Somerset and has Practiced Karate approximately 40 years. His father was an ex-boxer so from a very early age he encouraged the young Viv Nash to box. He boxed as a school-boy, teenager and as an adult. Joining the A.B.A. he fought in many competitions winning most of them. Later he boxed in fairground booths for 213 mins for three rounds; in those days he very much liked to fight, believing that boxing certainly helped the physical side of his Karate.

The next major step in his life was the British Army where he did 2 years National Service. He was still boxing and soon became Battalion Boxing Champion at Middleweight. While in the army, he was involved in a fire accident which effectively finished his boxing career.

After the army, he returned to his trade as a plumber, travelling to work on sites all over the country- which is how he eventually came to live and settle in Plymouth, Devon. It was there that he met a man called Dick Finnett, who was a Black Belt in Judo and taught a crude type of Karate. In those days, the late fifties, there was no organised Karate in Plymouth, so they practiced a real rough-house type of Karate- a bit of Karate, Judo and Boxing all mixed together! That was the start of his journey along the path of Karate-Do.

In the early sixties Dick Finnett had, at Sensei Harada's invitation, arranged a Karate course at Plymouth. Going along to this course, Viv Nash really had his eyes opened to what Karate was all about. At this time Mr Kanazawa started running courses at Plymouth, so one week Viv would practice with Sensei Harada, the next week with Sensei Kanazawa, so he was practising both Shoto-Kai and Shoto-Kan.

He found both Sensei's very good, but he came under the influence of Mr Harada because his Chi was very good, he would project his mind very strongly, so Viv practiced Shoto-Kai style and eventually became Club Instructor at Plymouth. Viv spent 18 years with the Shoto-Kai, going up through the grades and eventually being graded 4th Dan by Sensei Harada and was Chief Instructor at Plymouth as well as the Western Area Representative for Shoto-Kai.

It was in 1980 that, with great reluctance, Viv resigned from the Shoto-Kai; not because he fell out with Sensei Harada, but because of the way some of the Sensei Harada's senior students in one particular club. Within weeks, Plymouth and other western clubs also resigned.

In January 1981, a lot of club instructors and clubs that had resigned from the Shoto-Kai along with Viv, wrote to Viv to meet to decide their futures. Subsequently, a meeting was held in Plymouth- the outcome of which was that it was democratically voted to set up the Shoto-Ryu Karate Association and he was asked to become the Chief Instructor and Sensei. Feeling that this was the right step forward, he accepted and became a full time Sensei practising 7 days a week.

The main difference between Shoto-Ryu and other styles of Karate practice is that the style is very supple, the techniques are flowing, circular, dynamic movements.

The stop is not used, the breathing is not stopped and the punches are not jerked. Practitioners try to develop and project their minds and Ki energy; all techniques are flexible continuous movement; distance, speed, timing, and full use of the hips are very important. Kata, breathing and harmony play a big part in the practice. It was because of this similarity to Tai Chi that Viv Nash first got involved in this Chinese Martial Art.

He was graded 5th Dan in 1982 by an English Karate Committee but grades do not worry him. All he says is: 'Don't judge or assess me by my grade or what someone says I am, but come and practice with me, or watch my practice! That's my testimonial, not my grade I wear. Grades are not important, but what the message is that the teacher or instructor is trying to get over to the student is more important'.

(This testimonial you have read was taken from the website for the Shoto-Ryu Karate Kai).

In 1981 I started Under the Guidance of the Late Sensei 'Vivian Nash'.

Sensei Nash as I said earlier, in the book when I finished with Shotokai, he always had said I was treated badly by the Shotokai Administration, He always showed me great respect and had helped make up the lost time in my practice. Within Shoto-Ryu on many an occasion he complimented on the success of our club. I was awarded 1st Dan 1983, awarded 2nd Dan 1984 and awarded 3rd Dan 1987. From 1982 until 1993, I trained at all consecutive Summer Camps.

Picture by Richard Olpin.

I had such wonderful time's training with Sensei Nash. His testimonial, as we all know is his practice. Everybody will tell you that to practice with Sensei Nash, is and was a privilege; the respect, and admiration, of this man, goes far beyond just the way of practice and his teaching ability. The Shoto-Ryu was very much a family organisation, which contributed to the good sense of comradeship within the groups, which Sensei Nash always encouraged.

It is always easy to look back with hindsight to decisions you have made. One bad decision I made was breaking away from Sensei Nash and going out on my own, 'To Do My Own Thing', I look back and think of all the things I had missed with his teachings, and the comrade ship of being and training with Sensei Nash. This brought it home to me at his funereal, as I met old friends, his wife and family.

I was very moved, by his Grandson as he talked about his Granddad of how special he was. This was something we all had in common, and know that this man, 'Sensei Viv Nash', was a very special person, and will be missed by so many people. I would like to give these next pages, to a tribute to the memory of Sensei Viv Nash. As he will live forever, in the memories of everyone who knew him?

Sensei Viv Nash and some senior grade's on the beach in Devon.

Sensei Griffiths second right front row.

Grading panel at summer camp 1987. From the right Sensei Griffiths, Sensei Martin Turner.

Sensei Owen Lustcome, Sensei Barry Raftian, Sensei Viv Nash, Sensei Mike Crook.

Sensei Vivian Nash presenting me with my 2rd Dan Certificate, 1984.

Sensei Viv Nash in my garden at my home in Gloucester England.

48

Sensei Vivian Nash, doing a side kick from an attack of Oi zuki from Christopher May.

Sensei Vivian Nash, doing a flying kick to Christopher May's Izuki in my Garden.

Sensei Vivian Nash, doing a Flying Kick, against an attack with a Bokken from Sensei Raftian.

Sensei Viv Nash and Sensei Gerald Griffiths on the Canal bank at my home 13th June 1989.

Sensei Griffiths Sanchin Kata, Some wonderfull times we had on the Beach at summer Camp.

Sensei Vivian Nash demonstrating two-man set.

Two-man set of Tai-Ch.   **Sensei Nash deep in thought, having a rest.**

Sensei Viv Nash presenting Robert Huntley and Billy Griffiths,

with their 1st Dan Certificates.

Summer camp 1981, Sensei Viv Nash centre, Sensei Griffiths sitting between

Sensei Viv and Sensei Owen luscome. Second in from the right Sensei Barry Raftian.

I just had to put this picture in, as my Mum thought the world of Viv, even when I use to go to the home where she was before she died, we talked about Viv, and she always used to ask after him she would say, 'he's such a nice man'. I am sure she and Viv have met in that great world up yonder.

'GOD BLESS THEM BOTH'.

Chapter (9).   **Dedication to the Late Sensei Les Maclean.**

This photo 4th of May 2008.

To some up Sensei Les MacLean and how well he was liked, was the amount of people that came to his course's, and people on his mat, he would make martial arts fun, and that you were there to enjoy yourself, Sensei Les's Wife Vicky's words at his funeral said it all, he was a gentleman and true Welshman. Vicky was very kind to give permission to allow her Eulogy Letter in my book, of which she spoke of Les. You will now know what I am thinking, and the respect I have for; SENSEI LES MACLEAN.

Leslie Wavell MacLean Ll.M, B.A, PhD.
8th Dan Aikido, 7th Dan Judo, 4th Dan Karate, 2nd Dan Kendo,
1st Dan Iaido –Reiki Master Teacher
5th April 1940 – 30th March 2009

Although I write with great sadness I also have within me a great joy. Even though Les and I were together such a short time our life was filled with humour, music and a few "punch ups" as Les liked to call his martial arts seminars.

Les was a man of great intellect, huge generosity, fearless determination and gentle nature. He gave willingly of his time and energy to anyone with need of his help, he completed endless gradings without thought of taking a fee, and for myself Les gave me unconditional love, respect and a strong arm. He encouraged me to found my Reiki school and helped me with lesson plans and seminars. My husband my friend and mentor.

Now I must find my way back, I will remember all that he taught me (including Sankyo should I ever be faced with a mugger!) I will honour his memory by living life with dignity, humour and compassion.
Thank you for joining this celebration of his life.

In the words of Morihei Ueshiba founder of modern Aikido-1883-1969

"Daily training in the Art of Peace allows your inner divinity to shine brighter and brighter. Do not concern yourself with the right and wrong of others. Do not be calculating or act unnaturally. Keep your mind set on the Art of Peace, and do not criticize other teachers or traditions. The Art of Peace never restrains, restricts, or shackles anything. It embraces all and purifies everything".

Sensei's Wife Vicky Maclean's 'Eulogy'.

57

Sensei Les Maclean when he visited our club for our N.V.Q.'s

Sensei Robert Huntley receiving his fifth Dan from Sensei Les Maclean.

Gerald receiving an award for teaching on this seminar, 4th May 2008.

Sensei Les demonstrating a takedown from the Zen-Zon position with Sensei Bob Huntley.

Chapter (10)

On the courses within the Korekushon – Ju – Jitsu Association, I have had the respectful privilege of being able to instruct, with the invites by Sensei's Wayne Rice & Terry Boorer. Also from Sensei Billy Griffiths and his Clubs.

An Aikido take down technique, (Nikio), an awesome technique, which will simply push your opponent to the floor, right in front of you. Thanks to my partner, 'Kevin Goodby', in this picture, who is helping me in perfecting this technique?

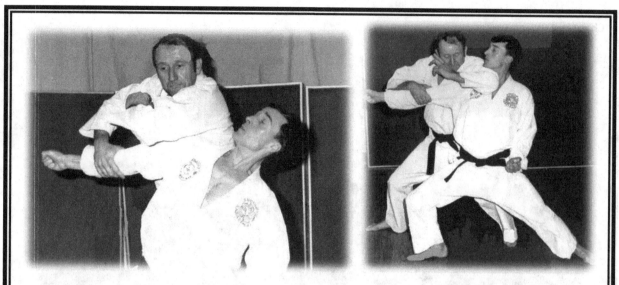

Blocking an Attack of Izuki and counter with elbow strike.

Blocking an Izuki and about to strike with Shoto-bari.

These photo's are photo's from an Ipon Kumite practice, which is a very important part of your practice, to be able to make the techniques work and become part of your being. All your techniques must be practiced diligently over and over. The practicality of self-defence only becomes possible by constant practice. With these practices confidence and the ability to stay calm in a dangerous situations, will become part of you and your safety.

Class of Special Constables under instruction by Mr. Bruce Sutherland. ("Daily Record" photo.)

These pictures are taken from, Mr Bruce Sutherland's Book of Ju-Jitsu Self-Defence.

There was no date on the book but it looks as though it goes back to almost 1940's 1950's. Being as there was no reference to copy-rights anywhere in the book. Credit to 'Daily record' photo, and Thomas Nelson and Sons Ltd.

By putting these pictures in, I wanted to show by these picture's to express how long Martial Arts has been about in Britain and other European Countries, and From those days, of how it has spread and became so popular throughout the World.

The following pictures were taken on the Butokukai Fellowship Course dedicated to Sensei Les Maclean.

This picture is Sensei (Skippy Brian Whipps demonstrating a take-down. Sensei Griffiths in background. As you can see Ju – jitsu and Akido has come a long, long way from those days in the fifties, you can see this in the demonstration picture's I have taken of Sensei Roy Smith 5th Dan from Birmingham, England.

This is Sensei Roy Smith 5th Dan, showing an Aikido technique, 'Ten-Kan-Shionage'.

In the picture Gerald & wife June with deadly Dicker, year 2000, I was entered, into the British Hall of Fame and was awarded, Dedicated Martial Arts Instructor of over thirty years.

Sensei Griffiths and some of the other award winners with Sensei Hopkin's, in 2002 awarded National Top Instructor of the year for my dedication and contribution towards Martial Arts in Gloucester and the U.K.

Chapter (11)

Left to right, B.K.J.A. Director in India. R. Sharma.

Sensei Gerald Griffiths was Director Tai-Chi, B.K.J.A. Area Director U.K and Chief instructor to The Shotos-traditional Karate-Kai

Sensei Kevin O'Connor, Chairman and founder of B.K.J.A.

Ahmed Ai-Houli, B.K.J.A. Director in Kuwait.

Sensei Robert Huntley, Second in Command to Shotos-Traditional-Karate -Kai

In 1999 we were affiliated to

The B.K.J.A. 'Bushi-Karate-Jitsu-Association', started with them in 1999 till 2008

Sensei Kevin O'Conner's ability and techniques were outstanding on the Mat. And thanks to Sensei Kevin O'Connor recognising us, and my ability to teach, we had become to be part of a well run organisation that was teaching Worldwide.

I was made Bushi-Karate-Jitsu-Association - Regional Director, and Technical Director for Tai-Chi.

A Course with the Bushi Karate-Jitsu Association 2000.

Typical Sensei Les taking a back step, hiding in the background.

In 1992, I started under the umbrella of Shikon

From 1992 until the present day, I started

'The Shoto's Traditional Karate-Kai'

'Was elected: The Chief Instructor'.

In 1994 was presented with my Award of 4th Dan.

In that same year Bob Huntley seen here in this picture, a picture of his physical and technical ability one of my most senior instructors.

Bob and myself with students from our club travelled to America with the Bushi Association in a teaching capacity. The tour was a big success and the chairman of Bushi Sensei Kevin O'Conner and founder of the Bushi Association said we had conducted ourselves so well and that the clubs that the Bushi delegates visited were very impressed with the standard of instruction by all.

Bob and I have also been on National T.V. showing our art, and as partners in Martial Arts, we are a force that can show the abilities of practice and practice.

Bob has shown me dedication and loyalty over thirty years, he has the ability to work hard and maintain a standard of fitness up and beyond the normal capacity of the average person. Bob's outstanding attention to detail and perfection shows in his work and in everything, he does.

One of the Senior Sensei's in America Sensei Edd Naumowicz nick-named Bob as Silent Bob and it has stuck. He is a quiet man, with a strong outward energy force. He presents confidence to the atmosphere of the Do-Jo. This confidence brings security in every outlook of his life. I am proud to be his teacher and friend. He is a good ambassador for the Martial Arts.

Sensei Robert Huntley just warming up and showing what hard practice & dedication can do.

Executive Instructor **Robert Huntley, his** Experience and Grades.

I have been practicing Martial Arts since 1979. Originally, I practiced the style of Shoto- Kai under the instruction of Sensei Harada and Sensei Griffiths as my Club Instructor but I have taken instruction from several organizations.

During my years of practice, I was fortunate to have been able to travel the country, attending numerous seminars and summer schools to improve my knowledge and experience gaining 1st and 2nd Dan with Shoto-Ryu based in Plymouth; a splinter group of Shoto-Kai; and 3rd Dan status gained from the Shi Kon organization.

My practice has not changed over the years but improved with the help of Tai Chi. this plays a very important part in my practice as it does in my everyday life. It helps me to relax and flow, has taught me to absorb energy and redirect it as well as generating strength.

Since joining the Bushi organization, I have gained valuable knowledge, experience, the opportunity to learn further new styles and have visited the United States with them to practice at various Do-Jo`. This has given me an insight into how other groups practice abroad. Within Bushi I also gained my 4th Dan status.

Karate Qualifications		Ju Jitsu Qualifications	
Orange belt	18/10/79	Red Belt	13/11/03
Green belt	25/09/80	Yellow Belt	12/05/04
Blue belt	21/12/80	Orange Belt	29/09/04
Brown Belt 3rd Kyu 20/05/81			
Brown Belt 1st Kyu 20/12/81		Karate Student of the Year Awards	
Black Belt 1st Dan 29/07/84		1980 1st Place	
Black Belt 2an Dan 29/08/87		1985 1st place	
1988 1st place			
Black Belt 3rd Dan 12/02/95		02-03 1st place	
Black Belt 4th Dan 28/04/02		03-04 1st place	
Black Belt 5th Dan 2010			
Regional Instructor Award 2003 – 3rd place. B.K.J.A. Open National			
Tai-Chi – over 20 years		Weapons – 1st place Kata – 3rd place	

Some great photos following, of the first trip to America.

The great times we had in America. This was at Sensei Bob Cook's club, Sensei Bob Cook centre with beard. Sensei Granville behind him with beard, Sensei Bob Huntley standing left. Sensei Griffiths on the right, Sensei O'Connor second left kneeling. Sensei Edd Naumowicz black Gi kneeling.

In a Bar called the other side in White-Haven left to right June. Edd, Gerald, Tony, Lee, Billy, and Kevin.

Gerald outside the Camp Ground of Edd's place.

Sensei's; Brad Hilderbrant, Bob Huntley, Edd Naumowicz, Gerald Griffiths, and Bob Cook, at Edds BBQ party at the Sandy Valley Camp Ground.

This is a Beautiful Lake on Eddy's Property, where I would run around it every day.

Gerald by Eddy's Lake, Sandy Valley Camp Ground.

Gerald and Bob doing a demonstration of Tai-Chi, for Grandmaster Nenow's Tournament.

The Tournament at Sensei Grandmaster Nennow's, Do'Jo.

The British Contingency, at Sensei Brad Hildabrant's club.

This is an amazing line up from the left, Sensei's Brad Hildabrant, Bob Cook, Edd Naumowicz,

Denny linch, Kevin O'connor, Gerald Griffiths, Billy Griffiths and Tom Hudaco.

From left to right: My wife, June Griffiths, Sensei Gerald Griffiths, and Grandmaster Nenow from America & Sensei Robert Huntley

Our second trip to America; after the first trip to America, some of the Sensei's out there was very impressed with what we had to offer. I was much taken aback when Edd Nomavech said he and some of the other Sensei's would like to ask us back, that is Robert Huntley and I. I would like to point out that without help from Robert Huntley my Student and partner it may not have happened; I am always able to put across what we are all about when Bob and I are working so well together.

Sensei Edd with Sensei Maryanne, and their daughter Julie.

So I was able to go back a few years later in 2007, and Sensei Edd Normavich made us so welcome, we visited quite a few clubs and they all made us very welcome, Sensei Bob Cook and Sensei Granville Steele allowed us to instruct at their clubs and especially made us welcome. I would like to say it was a very big privilege to be able to do so. At Bob Cooks club before I taught in the afternoon A Sensei from Philippines was teaching he was amazing he was seventy one years old and could move very quickly and his techniques were well executed.

My wife June actually wrote him a poem while she was watching him and gave it to him later at a Bar-b-Q in the evening; he loved it and said he would keep it and put it on his wall at his Do'Jo when he gets home. The actual day June wrote it was 3rd July 2007.as she always dates her poems

I quote; I met a very young man in Bob Cook's Martial Arts school. He was very fast and smooth and so real cool. He moved like a cat when teaching his techniques, cool and lean as he performed these feats.

He moved like grease lightning strong and fast as his opponents would hit the floor from his blows as they crashed.

This man I then found out was not so young. For all his life he trained for fun. His Martial arts kept him fit and toned, so his body was lean and very honed.

But this man was 71 his Martial Arts had kept him young.

His name was Bill and Uncle to you, what kept him young was Martial Arts and Kung Fu;

Bob and I each side of Sensei Uncle Bill. At Sensei Bob Cook's club, he is the Guy with the lighter beard directly behind Bob. Sensei Edd is the guy with the head scarf, behind Edd is Stein, who is now Edd's son-in-law married to Victoria, sitting on the floor behind the three children, is Julia, Edd other daughter, who is all grown up now and in the American Armed Forces,

Sensei Edd just thrown Stein, this is at Sensei Granvill Steel's club

Edd with the lads.

Photo by Edd Naumowicz

I just had to put this picture in, this is Sensei Edd Naumowicz with his two daughters, Victoria, and Julie, Julie being in the Armed Forces, two very strong minded girls who I know Edd is very proud of, they are a credit to Edd and Maryanne. Edd hosted our trip to America and looked after us so well, I am honoured to be his friend. I look forward so much to returning to America and seeing them all again.

Whilst there in America, America being very gun orientated and in Pennsylvania guns are in abundance, which is redneck type of country, we were not very far away from the Poconos mountains, we were near a town called White Haven, on Eddy's place The Happy Valley Camp Ground.

Edd took us out for a target Shoot, up in the Poconos Mountains, and to get there we had to drive along a forest trail deep in these mountain hills, we then had to go by foot to where the shoot would take place.

When we were going through the wood we came to a wide stream coming out of the wood, and would have to cross a fiord were it was shallow, I step on to stones in the shallows and immediately felt a blast of cold air coming out of the forest, on my left as I turned to see where it was coming from, deep in the wood I could see a cave.

Edd told me that it was a coal mine, and with the up draft and cold water coming out of the mine it was like a natural air conditioner, it was really weird, I stepped back I was warm as it was summer and like Australia it can become very hot and humid, when I step forward I was cold one step back and one step forward, hot and cold. We got where we were going, and Stein one of the lads started to unload the guns I was very astonished at how many, there was Ak 7.62 Ak 47, Magnum revolver and rifle, and shotguns, it was crazy and a great experience you could only imagine. Of course ex-Grenadier and all that, I was a good shot and they were impressed.

Wesley Tasker, Stein, Edd Julie and Victoria

Met a guy at Bob Cook's club he had an arsenal of guns this is me posing with one.

Which looks very similar to the SLR?

Chapter (12) # Teaching and instruction Techniques.

My Philosophy in teaching as a Martial Arts Instructor.

I have always encouraged my student's sense of individuality and have treated them as equals. I have learned that a competent teacher is particularly important to a first grader, for this is the foundation to his Karate-Do, (Tai Chi). I try to remember that a student's imagination extends far beyond their capability and knowledge; therefore I try to help bring him/her into the right perspective.

Most actions that are repeated regularly become a habit. Good character is a habitual tendency to act wisely and well, and naturally a good instructor wants his students to be of good character.

I instruct my students to be pleasing and agreeable in relationships with others, and at the same time, be admired, trusted and respected at all times, 'not just in the do-jo'.

An instructor has a good chance of establishing deeply and firmly good straits of character and disposition in the minds of his pupils.

When we practise, we must look to the present and the future and meditate on the past. Remember that it is not the amount of books you read sermons you hear and courses you attend but the frequency and earnestness with which you meditate and practise them until the truth and understanding of them becomes your own and part of your being.

'A page digested is better than a volume hurriedly read'. *(Macaulay).*

I try not to curb a student's initiative and get him to answer some of his own questions, remembering too little guidance results in feelings of inadequacy and a lack of self-confidence.

The more I think of my faults and feelings, the harder becomes my teaching. I put my own feeling aside out of consideration for my pupil. I teach my students to approach new situations without anger or fear, and try to face and overcome them.

My Son, Graham Griffiths on my Left. On my Right, Nick king, and Miss Fletcher.
Front row, Richard king, Ian Jenkins, Graeme Fletcher, Ian Frazier.

I try to find faults with myself constantly; I believe the greatest of faults is to be conscious of none. If all my faults were written on my head, I would never take my hat off. We should correct our own faults by seeing how unseemly they appear in other people. *(Writer Unknown)*

'It is not so much the being exempt from faults as having overcome them that is an advantage to us, it being with the follies of the mind as with the weeds of a field, which if destroyed and consumed upon the place of their birth, enrich and improve it more than if none had ever sprung there.' *(POPE)*

Practicing the one side of a two man set.

'Cultivate consideration for the feelings of other people if you would not have your own injured'. *(Righter)*

'The more you practise what you know the more shall you know what to practise? *(W. Jenkin)*.

A line up in Zen-Zon at Quedgeley Karate Club, Gloucester, England, Sensei Philip knickenberg taking class

'STUDYING YOUR STUDENT'.

The more I read and understand N.V.Q`s, the more I realise that I have been getting it right with my own teaching over the years.

(Of which I now have T.D.L.B standard in N.V.Q. Qualifications at level 3 as a Vocational Assessor for Sports Coaching (Combat Arts) by Completing Units D32- assessment through Observation A D33 – Assessment by Diverse means)

The Butokukai Fellowship Trust
&
North Midlands Aikikai
In conjunction with the
OPEN COLLEGE NETWORK
Certify that

GERALD GRIFFITHS

Has shown competence against TDLB standards
In NVQ level III as a

VOCATIONAL ASSESSOR
for
SPORTS COACHING (COMBAT SPORTS)
By completing Units

D 32 - Assessment through observation
D33 - Assessment by diverse means

Signed
Dr L W MacLean LLm., B.A.
for the awarding body

Date: 4th June 2005

N.V.Q. Certificate

My standard of teaching has been quite high and I have always kept my honour and principles when grading, and I am sure that I have been able to keep my students respect.

You can see my standard in my most senior students, Bob Huntley to name one.

I am sure that Bob would never have stayed with me so long if I had not induced the standard that we have to this very day.

Now that Bob Huntley and I have become Assessors, I am sure that standard will remain, and that as a group we will become an asset to the N.V.Q. management strata of the organisation of our Group.

Personally as a conscientious coach, I have always made a selfless concentrated effort on the development of an individual and our group.

When studying my students today (our Black Belts), I know my efforts were worthwhile and they are now my best friends on whom I can rely on in anyway.

I know the ability to apply past experience is vital to learning. When a student learns new Kata`s, he/she should be able to have the ability if he/she" practises regularly, to solving new techniques and problems in new Kata's.

In addition; if the instructor can give effective satisfying results when demonstrating techniques, constantly supervise and never letting a wrong fault go unnoticed and remember that each student's rate of speed in learning is different. In addition, always be constructive when giving guidance, always considering your student's ability then he/she will always improve.

Sensei Gerald Glyn Griffiths

& Lord Mayor & his Lady, of Stoke on Trent.

'To be vain of one's rank or place is to show that one is below it'. *(Stanislaw)*

Within Shotos Traditional Karate Kai, every aspect is considered and planed with a new student in mind.

Particular attention should be paid to a new student, to interacting him or her to the way we practice.

Training can be individually tailored for students with a one to one tuition, which is structured to ensure that each student can make the most of the available technology of techniques on daily basis. An Instructor on passing on instruction to another instructor on that student's progress, so they can follow on from the last practice he/she was practicing. If the student keeps asking questions of that instructor, it should encourage that instructor to find satisfactory answers.

Sensei Griffiths, assisting a Student the Late Tony Neary to block a Downwards block from Sensei Huntley's Oi'zuke. Tony Neary was a great student: But sadly he was killed in a car accident on the way to work. R.I.P. 'Tony Neary'.

An instructor must set standards of ethics for his students that are better and more effective than preaching, by setting examples of his own conduct and manner. Conflict and differences of opinion between instructors must be hammered out in private, and not in the dojo; unnecessary noise and talking must be kept to a minimum. When practice has started never let members (non-members) in and out of the Dojo unnecessarily.

I will now write many of the things Karate/Tai-Chi can and does develop by good instruction.

Honesty, Humility, leadership, loyalty, Obedience, Patience, Perseverance, Punctuality, Kindness, Integrity, Helpfulness, Friendship, Effort, Good Manners, Courtesy, Courage, Co-operation, Contentment, Concentration, Cleanliness, Caution, Ambition, Accuracy, Tolerance, Wisdom, They are not put in order of preference, for everyone is important. There are many more, but these are just some, and if we ponder, read, discuss and practise them, our karate, and combat arts, and instruction will be for the better.

This is Sensei teaching a blind man, this is where the practice and sensitivity comes in where the person needs to make contact and through body movement, you first feel the feeling through the sensitivity of the fingers and six-sense and the awareness of everything about you.

Chapter (13)   **STUDENTS UNDERSTANDING OF TECHNIQUES**

You must remember as an instructor you are there for the benefit of the student.

It is all right to show a student this technique or that technique, but you must also get him to understand the technique, so a good instructor must have the ability to demonstrate effectively.

After demonstrating, always asks the class for questions, did they understand the demonstration? If you do not keep this in mind your students will become like robots, they will be thrusting, kicking back and forth, not knowing what they are doing wrong.

If you give them good understanding of the technique when demonstrating, you will find they will be able to look at themselves critically.

Sensei Gerald Griffiths, teaching Tai Chi at a seminar at Stoke-on-Trent.

So we have established and come to a conclusion, to understand a technique given by an instructor we must observe the technique exactly." If in doubt ask".

Point out to a tall and a short student how to adjust to the others height. Many mistakes in combat arts are caused by lack of understanding. Remember mistakes, we all make them.

Here I will write the thoughts and philosophy of two great people;

"To make no mistakes is not in the power of man, but from their errors

And mistakes, the wise and good learn wisdom for the future". "Plutarch".

"Experience teaches slowly and at the cost of mistakes". "Froude"

Always remember when practising; never be in conflict with each other, but practise in harmony with mind, body and breathing. You must look on your partner not only as a fighting opponent, but also as a practising partner to help each other.

Demonstrating

First, when demonstrating do a complete demonstration "how it should be done (quickly)". Then do it slowly, and ask questions

Then break the techniques into parts, show and explain each part.

Now get your class to do each part exactly and slowly. After they have begun to get better, do the completed technique all the way through, (still slowly).

Do it that much quicker as more confidence is shown by your class.

Make sure that your students understand fully before allowing them to go on

Gerald showing how to get out of a strangle hold.

Showing how to get out of a strangle hold.

Always strive for perfection in all your practice, although you find some things unattainable, aim at it and persevere and you will come nearer to finding it than those who give up easily.

Remember a purpose can be the eternal constitution of success.

Modern day Karate is put into categories, a martial art, a sport, and self-defence. I think that if you practice as a sport or for self-defence that is all you will get from it.

However, if you practice it as an art you will find the other two will follow automatically and you will find many more things, and meliorate from them.

People of a criminal character will not find the true way of Karate, which is primarily, mastery of your-self.

To begin with, the training seems senseless and requires lots of stamina, the basic schooling and the basic techniques in karate takes many months, in some cases years, so the bullies and people of bad character drop out after only a few lessons.

'The wise man endeavours to shine in himself, the fool to outshine others. The first is humbled by their own infirmities and the other is lifted up by the discovery of those, which he observes in other men. The wise man is happy when he gains his own approbation and the fool when he recommends himself to the applause of those about him'.   ("Addison")

Sensei Griffiths, at the Ladies self-defence class

demonstrating blocking a knife attack from his wife June.

Striking & breaking the leg same time,

Chapter (14)

Distance, timing, harmony, & 'Movements during Kimuta'.

When facing each other for escape, the importance of, (D.A.T.E.), DISTANCE, ANTICIPATION, TIMING, and ESCAPE, if you keep your distance correct and find correct timing, you can take the initiative when your partner's harmony and discord collapses. You pursue and keep pursuing, but if negligent he will recover.

This is the distance, timing and rhythm in strategy. You must know your partner's timing and distance in order to understand your own.

With a keenness of eye and the ability to move your body in co-ordination with decisive moves with your opponent, you will find your opponent's weaknesses.

If your distance is correct, (Ma-Ai Distancing) there will be no need to block your partner. First, you must allow for the height of your partner. Adjusting your distance so that his kick or oi-zuki is just out of reach, you can then counter. At all times in your practice, act naturally and be calm, if not you will get tense and stiff. Movements during kimute, are moving constantly strategically inducing unwanted movement in your opponent in order to break his structure and concentration. When there is a sign of inattentiveness, once weak, you can then attack, you're constantly looking for his breathing cycle, for when he cannot transmit or use his own force,

Keep your own breathing cycle hidden. Keeping your power and centre in your (tanden) lower centre of the stomach. Keep at least a third of your breath, for sudden unwanted movements from your opponent.

Ladies Self-Defence Class; Sensei Griffiths showing one of the Ladies how to get out of a strangle hold. You can see the love and admiration of his wife June, the one with her hands clasped under her chin.

Sensei Griffiths, with a Side Kick against an attack,

From Sensei Steve Walker.

Try to pace your movements in a controlled manner, whilst trying to make your opponent break his concentration or alter his breathing pattern.

When his mouth opens and he starts to breath from the chest, is the time to attack. His body condition will change from fighting to withdrawing, attacking at this time as he breathes in. Keeping your mind totally mentally focused (Zanshin). Not allowing your mind to wander and be distracted.

You must practice this regularly to understand it fully. It is not the winning that is important when practicing, but the way in which you win.

The do in Karate-Do means the way and Karate means empty hand, so it is not Karate that is important but the way. This is in all things you must search for the way, and then you can understand Karate-Do

'If a little knowledge is dangerous where is the man who has so much as to be out of danger'? 'THOMAS. H. HUXLEY'.

Man can never come up to his ideal standard. It is the nature of the immortal spirit to raise that standard higher and higher as it goes from strength to strength, still upward and onward. The wisest and greatest of men are ever the most modest.   'S.N.F. OSSOLI'.

Sensei Griffiths Sparring in Australia

Wayne Scott's Clubs of Taekwondo in Eagle Vale, near Camden Town.

Sensei Wayne was kind enough to allow Sensei Gerald Griffiths,

to teach his karate at his various clubs of Taekwondo

'What we know here is very little, but what we are ignorant of is immense'. 'Laplace'.

These quotations throughout my writings, I have chosen with great care to express the true meaning of Karate-Do and my own feelings and thoughts on my own practice.

If an instructor studies and meditates on them, he/she should then find a better relationship with his/her students; they will admire and trust, him/her. By gaining there trust and admiration, pupil and instructor will improve more quickly.

'Zanshin'.

In sparing (kimute) or in a life threatening situation, to have a strong sense of Zanshin, is, or can be the automat senses.

The Zanshin mean's one's total awareness, it is never achieved though annualizing, but must be found by constant practice of physical and mental practices. An intense use of the sense's and calmness of your mind without anger or fear. To achieve this proper physical and mental attitude, is to practice, is so important to finding a six sense. The same as a warrior would think and feel, 'no mind'.

A teacher can never give you these six senses by word alone, only you can find this from just practice, there is no mind between the tips of each other's sword, feet, or hands as you face an adversary.

My teacher, Sensei Vivian Nash, years ago, used to talk to me as we went through a form, and ask me questions, I use to find it very difficult and hard to be able to answer him, because from concentrating on the form, and what I had to do, and to answer him at the same time was difficult.

He said the day you can talk and do the form the same time, and then you are fully aware of your practice and your own ability.

The same as you face an adversary you should be able to keep the same mind, not just to be able to concentrate on one thing but all of your surroundings and adversary at the same time.

This is the same mind as no mind between two Samurai Warriors and the tips of both of their sword.

If all your different practices were all different colours, then you keep practicing and when you find and see only one colour, then you will understand this concept, when you see this one colour, then, practice, practice, and practice. YOU WILL THEN FIND ENLIGHTENMENT.

When I was in the armed forces on Manoeuvres in British Guiana, as it was called then and after their independence, called Guyana.

 I was in the interior of the Forrest canopy. The Forrest canopy is so dense and dark just like night time, you could not see the sky. Yet it was day time with the sun shining hot outside of the jungle, what with the condensation dripping down from the tops of the trees, the tree being hundreds of feet high it would be almost like rain where it was so wet and hot.

Anyway, the interior was so dense as you creep through, trying not to make a sound but listening for the enemy. You feel your breathing, but trying not to even allowing your breath to be heard, breathing through the mouth, which is less noisy, listening to every sound.

Everything is magnified in this situation, so all your senses must come into focus, not just concentrating on any one thing, but on everything that you possibly can. 'Which again is no mind', you never focus on any one thing, but all things at the same time, the rustle of leaves, the mouse or snake, rat, or even small insects on the ground, you can here every sound there is, the smell the intense heat and condensation that is all around you.

In this condensed atmosphere the enemy may only be feet away and you would not know it, so this no mind is so important; 'No mind yet aware of everything'. This could save your life someday, even as just going out for the evening, just being aware of what you are doing, and the people around you, have you had too much to drink, are you in control of all your faculties.

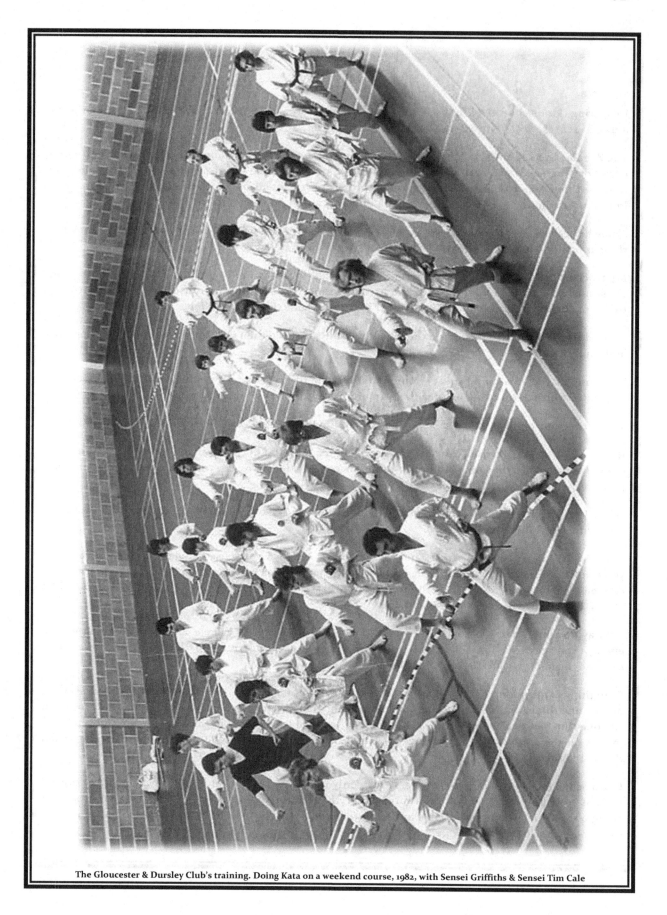

The Gloucester & Dursley Club's training. Doing Kata on a weekend course, 1982, with Sensei Griffiths & Sensei Tim Cale

Chapter (15).

TAI CHI & KATA.

Most people experience stress differently from person to person, and some of the causes of stress can be from the pressures of the work place, or for caring for others, taking on too much, and the feeling that you can't cope, not having support when you need it.

The feelings need to become balanced, some stress in our lives can be benefited, and essential, to motivation, and can be helpful to you.

However, excessive stress can be harmful, and can affect your physical and emotional wellbeing.

Stress and the way you react to it, it is essential to allow time to unwind after a hard day learning to relax every day. Keeping a daily routine and being organised helps. If it is stress at work, seek advice.

Remember your Employer has a legal responsibility about reasonable workloads, talking with friends and family is helpful.

Nevertheless, the main distress-err is soft exercise. From my years of experience in Martial Arts, Karate and Tai Chi has been one of the best forms of relaxing stress.

In Karate, we have Kata, and when we practice, our Karate movements with in the style, it is the same as Tai Chi, as you will see in this chapter.

The main Kata's of our group are:

Taikyoku; Shodan, Nidan, Sandan, (The first cause).

Heian; shodan, Nidan, Sandan, Yodan, Godan, (peaceful mind).

Bassai; (to penetrate a fortress).

Kwanku; (To look at the Sky).

Empi (flying swallow).

Gankaku; (crane on a rock).

Jutte; (Ten hands).

Hangetsu; (half-moon).

Tekki; (Horse riding).

Jion; (join-Ji is a famous old temple).

Ten no Kata (The kata of the universe).

Taikyoko Shodan Kata.

(1)Yoi Ready stance.   (2) Step left (A) Gedan Barai .   (3) Front stance (B) Gedan Barai.

(4) Chudan Oi-zuke front stance.   (5) Step back right foot turn.   (6) Gedan Barai front stance.

(7) Step left foot, Chudan O-zuke.   (8) Left foot Step to left. (9) Gedan Barai. (10) Chudan O-zuke.

95

(11) Step left foot Chudan O-zuke. (12) Step right foot Chudan-Ozuke with Kai. (13) turn anticlockwise.

(14 Into Gedan Barai.   **(15) Step with right Chudan O-zuke.**

(16) Step back right foot into Gedan Barai. (17) Step left foot Chudan O-zuke. (18) Turn to Left.

(19) Gedan Barai left.   **(20) (21) (22) Three Chudan O-zuke's.**   **(22) Kai, last punch.**

(23) (A) Anticlockwise Turn Gedan Barai.   (24) (B) Gedan Barai.   **(25) Chudan O-zuke.**

(26) (A) Turn Step back right foot.   (27) (B) Gedan Barai.   **(28) Step Chudan O-zuke.Step up**

Left foot into Yoi ready stance.

Demonstrated by Ian Parry.

Kata Direction

The Pattern showing the direction

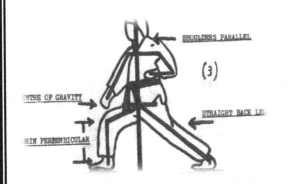
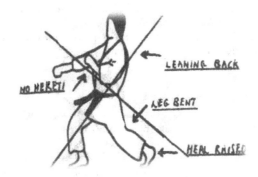

Right and Wrong of posture

In these kata's, it is very important to fully understand the three points of the main factors of the particular Kata's. You need to look at your speed strength and expansion, and contraction, of your body movements. You have to study all and each particular significance of each technique. Remember not to be taken in by excessive rapid movements of strength, because this really is no indication of skill.

You must study when you need rapid movements, or when you need speed. Although are movements are a continuous flow, with quite relaxed flowing moves, in the various given kata's you need to know when to apply the strength, slow moves and the fast flowing movements at the right moments.

Within our Tai Chi, the Long Yang has continua's moves from start to finish, inducing relaxation.

Where the Cheng has fast and slow moves with very explosive rapid movements with strength.

The explosive moves come from the hips, which is a violent hip movement, (Fa-Ching).

The speed of your form will, or can dictate your breathing circle in the utilisation of your hips.

The importance of the retraction of your back hand (Eki-tai) is just as important as your forward attacking hand (Mai-Tai)

Within the Chinese writings of Chi-kung and Tai Chi forms, it does come across as though it is all mystiques and some form of secret technique, but from my own practices and I hope from all my explanations, and writings, we can raise above this ball, and find what is in all of us, and within all our own capabilities.

So by studying these factors you will fully understand your kata's, and by looking at the respective stances and your posture. Posture being one of the most important factors of kata. Without good posture, you will lose all the other important factors.

You need to look at the line of movements of your kata's and study the line of the direction exactly.

These lines are so important to the particular kata you are performing. The groups of lines are very important and consist of five particular lines. You need to study these five lines on or before you begin to start your form, to know where to stand at the starting point. You must visualise the form in your mind. As an instructor, it is very important, to point this out to your pupil.

All these lines are showing the correct direction of the kata's. As a student, progresses, there are differences' in the higher kata's, being of more complicated move and lines, like the lines of kwanku-dai and Gankaku. Then there are the strait lines of the Tekki kata's.

By keeping to these exact lines, you will find that when you finish, you should always return to the same spot exactly where you started. Therefore, your steps should be correct every time.

In practicing the kata's the main benefits is the stimulation of mental and physical relaxation. The mental stimulation is having to remember all about your movements, learning, and memorizing all the patterns and forms. The relaxation is when you are going through the forms having to concentrate your thoughts, thus diverting your thoughts away from your worries of your daily life.

Obviously the memorisation of the Kata movements are very important, as, if you don't memorise them you can't perform your Kata, nevertheless it is extremely important to be able to perform the techniques in a combat situation, and to have full understanding of the individual techniques. The self-defence of each technique is more important as well as the flowing movement aspect of the Kata's. But as I said, you need to get it flowing to understand and relax the body as you perform your Kata, and if you practice diligently, you will find in a group, or with a partner, that you need to make every move an individual technique of your very own.

After practicing Kata and getting it to flow, you need to practice your Ten no Kata with the same dexterity and commitment, searching for good technique. I have read somewhere that the translation for finding distance and timing in Japanese is the word MAOI. This is the timing and distance in your kumite, understanding the speed of your opponent, MAOI is the automat timing of moving in to your opponent. Finding the nucleus and mental attitude and the centre in your gravity in the hara you should be able to conquer yourself and your weaknesses therefore, developing your character.

Hopefully I have been able to put across that the training of the mind to becoming a better person is just as important as building your techniques

With the longer Kata's you will find, if done slowly you will find the same relaxation as people that find relaxation in their practice of Ta-Chi.

By fixing on their long sequence, in Kata and Tai-Chi, especially forms of the Cheng and long yang of Tai Chi, being so complexes and long, your relaxation and stimulation, the benefits will be so beneficial and affective.

Thinking cannot be clear till it has had expression. We must write, speak, or act our thoughts, or they will remain in a half-torrid form. Our feelings must have expression or they will be as clouds, which until they descend in rain, will never bring up fruit or flowers. So it is with all inward feelings, expression gives this development. 'H.B. Beecher'.

This is something to remember when practicing Tai Chi or Kata.

Appreciation of nature gives a student spiritual values, and teaches him more about living. Kata and Tai Chi can do the same.

They express all a student should see, feel and think. You can then observe his character through physiognomy.

By observing others doing Tai Chi, and Kata, he/she will learn about themselves. As he/she learns about themselves, he/she gradually builds their own standard of values; a good instructor will help, guide and build this standard.

He/she learns through Karate, Tai-Chi, that other people, like themselves are faced with the same problems of working out their feelings of security and self-respect, he/she will not find a perfect world, but it is a world to which he/she can add his/her bit in helping others towards a happy and useful life.

A quotation that again comes to mind is from, 'Cranch'.

Thought is deeper than all speech; feeling deeper than all thought; soul to souls can never teach what unto them-selves was taught. 'Cranch'.

TAI-CHI, is becoming very popular, but again and again teacher's are finding that beginner students lose their interest after only a few lessons, because they despair because of the many techniques they must learn.

However' if a student is taught to achieve the correct point of view, and studies diligently, he/she will find similarities repeatedly between the various techniques.

If you explain this, he/she on finding this will realise that, (TAI-CHI) & (KATA), as a whole is no longer a large collection of techniques.

My Son Graham doing a side kick on the heavy bag.

The overall view is that you no longer find it so long and hard. They then can make the techniques their very own; this will come with regular practice.

And with regular practice and self criticism looking again and again at them/selves doing TAI-CHI & KATA, they improve. There is no promise that you will master TAI CHI, & KATA, in a short time, but with understanding and self-criticism. You will find enlightenment.

Tai Chi is one of the best ways of finding body management. The hundred – twenty one moves of the Long-Yang, I think is the best form to start with. The Long –Yang takes twenty to forty minutes to perform. The slower the performance through proper control, the greater the benefits of well being.

You can find inner peace of mind, with a qualified teacher, and by practicing diligently, Tai Chi is the best form of exercise to revitalize and awaken every cell in your body, especially in a sick body.

All movements must be practiced harmoniously and with a rhythmic continuous movement.

Important principles of the art are relaxation; movements should be circular and relaxed with soft movements from one to the other in a continuous flow without pauses.

The head, body, arms, legs and eyes should be well co-ordinated

Do not let your body rise and fall abruptly, move at a slow even pace, all breathing is performed through the nose; your breathing is natural and breathing through the diaphragm (lower Tan-tien. To search for a strong Chi you need to think positive, guiding your mind.

Your Chi energy will flow during the entire form and you will have meditation in motion.

Tai Chi as a whole within itself is perfectly balanced and will rebalance your whole system when practiced regularly. All of us can get backache at some time; usually it is because we do not think of our backs in everyday life, until it causes us a problem.

The importance of a good poster is preserving the natural shape of our backbone. As in Tai Chi, it is important for a correct posture on lifting and moving in your everyday life.

Gentle calm movements, which stretch the body, will leave you feeling relaxed and aware of your body poster. Tai-Chi should not become a time consuming ritual that becomes a burden so just a few moves a day, when you have ten or twenty minutes to spare, usually in the mornings is the best time.

After just a few days, you should start to feel the benefits that Ta-Chi can give.

Of course, Tai Chi was originally a Chinese fighting art, it relies on the softness, and sensitivity rather than aggression, instead of meeting force with force you yield taking the energy away from your opponents attack putting him off balance. This is the real emphasis of self-defence.

Whatever your strategy or thoughts in Kata/Tai-Chi; Remember:

'The nerve which never relaxes- the eye which never wanders, the purpose that never wavers, these are the masters of victory'.
"Aaron".

Participants need to concentrate fully on the forms and movements (patterns). Ignoring any out-side interference to reach a state of inner-peace and fulfilment within the body.

Giving you complete therapeutic meditation.

In Karate it has been known for people to break tiles. I would like to point out that this really has nothing to do with Karate, and the accomplishments of good Karate concepts of learning. Nevertheless, to be able to brake, it do's take a positive mind to do this (it do's hurt) and you have to change that particular emotion into a focused concentration into the brake.

I know I keep repeating the fact that I am trying to hopefully, put across that the training of your mind in your practices, is to become a good person, as much as the importance of the physical techniques.

I am trying to put across the training of teaching beyond the techniques to character building of your students. Try to give young students the hope for the future, is through hard work in all they do, and with a positive mind to overcome all obstacles which is ever put their way. Always teach them to be well mannered and respectful to their elders and opinions of other people.

These were the very strong character building elements that I had learnt within the Grenadier Guards.

You must give this positive well-mannered attitude of respect to your elders and people around you.

'THEN YOU WILL GET IT IN RETURN'.

Some of my writings that I have been showing in this book, is all about the qualities of finding your energy, focus, and concentration of your Ki, and of presenting your aura, it is a very hard quality to find, but there is a lot of people in Martial Arts that has and can find these qualities.

I was at a Competition around 2005; I was watching this young lad of around only seven years old, as he was doing his Kata in the Competition. The Kata was outstanding, and he presented the kata with so much concentration. His aura was full of energy; in as much as any adult that I have ever seen.

In this competition he easly walk away with the first top prize of Best Kata in the competition.

What made him stand out was not just his excelent techniques, but this sense of concentration, in such a young boy. His name was, 'Brookln Peckham', from Cardiff, Wales, England.

Later in the competition when the adult's started their category, I soon realised where he got it from, like Father, like Son. His father, 'Carl Peckham', was in the same competition. Carl Peckham' he also has this same aura about him, his Martial Arts is so outstanding, both father and son has these same qualities

Remembering my own son, 'Graham John Griffiths, these same qualitys he also had, and on looking back on my teachings, I now remember how hard I was on him, as he was my son, and I wanted him to be the best, so I used to make him work harder than the rest of my students.

Carl, is the nices person you could possibly meet, for a father and son to have these same interest in Karate and the strong influance he had for his son, which go's far beyound, the respect and admiration of a father and his son, is something to be admirerd.

As well as Carl Peckham and his son, I am sure that the respect and admiration, that my son and I have, as he was growing up has been through the Martial Arts, that we practiced together, as well and of course trying to be a good father, and not just his instructor in Martial Arts.

Brooklyn Peckham, and his Dad,
Carl Peckham, doing sidekicks.
(Yoko Geri Kekomi Jodan).

'The photos says it all'.

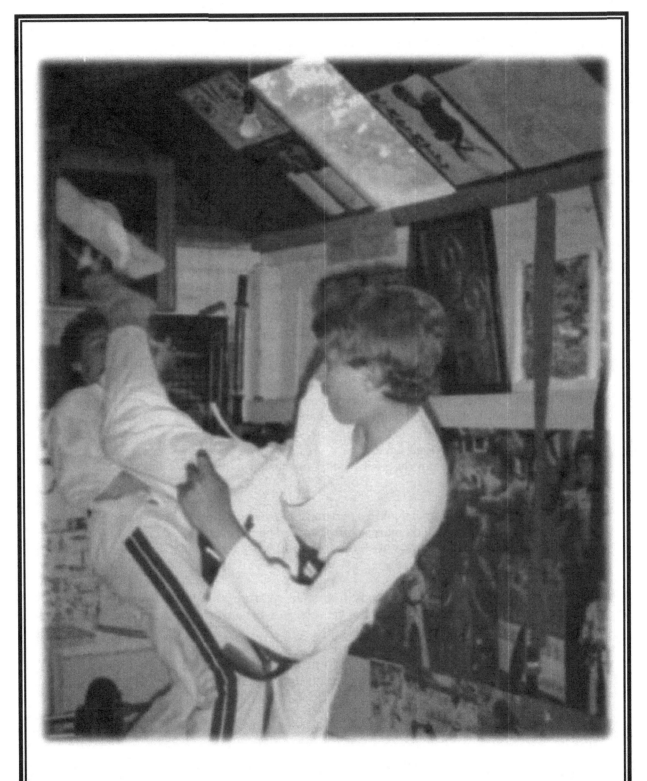

This is my Son Graham, age 14 years old sparring with Dean George. Graham had some wonderful training sessions with Dean around that time. This was in our old Gym at the Rea Bridge House in Gloucester, before the new one was built.

Chapter 16

The philosophy of physical, mental and spiritual dimensions based on teaching and understanding the Ki`Ai within the martial arts

The Ki`ai in martial arts is one of the key elements of obtaining strength and energy and contributing to circulating your Chi energy through out your body. This is the shout, which a practitioner gives, on focus of a punch, or kick, "with their opponent".

Some of the ways that I can explain about the Ki`ai in the martial arts. Two dogs, or two cats, are faced off for a fight, also a snake, stags, (Deer) and most animals.
 As they face each other, two dogs will be growling, so whilst growling they are breathing out.
Two cats will be doing the same, they will be hissing and spitting at each other, so again will be breathing out. The snake as he raises his head he is also hissing, and breathing out,

Going back to the dogs, "if you picture the two dogs as they fight", "you will get the picture". As they are fighting they are growling, barking, and snapping, this makes them strong expanding and exploding which is intercepting energy, (Chien-Chin) which is the main elements in combat.
Most fighting soldiers within the military make this Ki ai, this gives them courage, energy, and also frightens, and startles the enemy as they make their charge from their foxholes, (trenches). Indian's will completely do the same as they whop and holler around the wagon train on their horses.
 A paratrooper jumping from the plane will shout, as he falls through the sky, this will give him courage.

Within a human element and thinking person, this can be harnessed in a positive way where a person can also rely on more subtle means. The push hands exercises is all about sensitivity allowing your partner to move in a relaxed and efficient manner both are practicing balance, relaxing tense areas

Then you can build up to push hands free style sparring, this is free – flowing and continuous, learning to pull your punches yet focusing the power where ever you direct it and absorbing blows from your opponent.

 This practice needs some supervision, so both students are working at a safe speed and control, at a safe level, with the minimum of tension with a mind to over come force and fear.

Within our group, I have encouraged personal self-paced programs with maximum results. No one practice of training is of benefit, but all our programs put together, provides the results in pinpointing weaknesses within a student's body, this then can be concentrate on..

This was a student who trained with me a few years ago in 1987; 'Richard Olpin'. Who is showing a strong Ki-ai, in his Facial expressions. He is now a Sensei of his own successful group.

The ki-ai this is the concentrated energy which we emit when we need extra energy to do something.

Heavy lifting, pushing, or pulling, this surge of power comes from the breath in your body as you breathe out or grunts or groan as you lift.

The potential of one's internal powers are far and way beyond our own imagination. This power can be released by fear anger and determination, to do something that you want to do.

It has been known where a frail small women has lifted and turned a car over because there child was trapped underneath. Where did all that energy come from?

This Ki-ai is the internal energy we all have, which is all to do with chi energy, which circulates our bodies, which can come to the fore, weather it is yourself, or your loved one's life's that is in danger, the psychological and physiological will give up that energy, which is far above the normal ability in your everyday lives.

The self protecting limits of are every day duties of overexertion and extreme strain and fatigue will not allow this underutilization of power as a normal thing. If these self protections were not in place, we would be in danger of doing ourselves extreme harm of life threatening injuries and of over exertions of health threatening mental and physical harm.

Photo by Richard Olpin

Sensei Robert Huntley

Sensei Richard Olpin

A very young Sensei Griffiths and a young sensei Bob Huntley.

Chapter (17)

(1)   (2)   (3)

(1)	Up right posture.-------------
(2)	Complementary Bow.------
(3)	Step forward right (Hour--Glass) Sanchin Dachi Double Ude Uki.

(4)   (5)   (6)

(4)	Middle punch left side.
(5)	Hand goes back to (Ude-Uki) middle block.
(6)	Step forward left, (Hour Glass) Sanchin Dachi, keep Ude-Uki still.

(7)   (8)   (9)

(7)	Middle punch right side.
(8)	Hand goes back to middle block.
(9)	Step forward right, (hour Class) Sanchin Dachi, keep Ude-Uki still.

(10)   (11)   (12)

(10)	Punch left side.
(11)	Back to double Ude-Uki
(12)	Punch right side

108

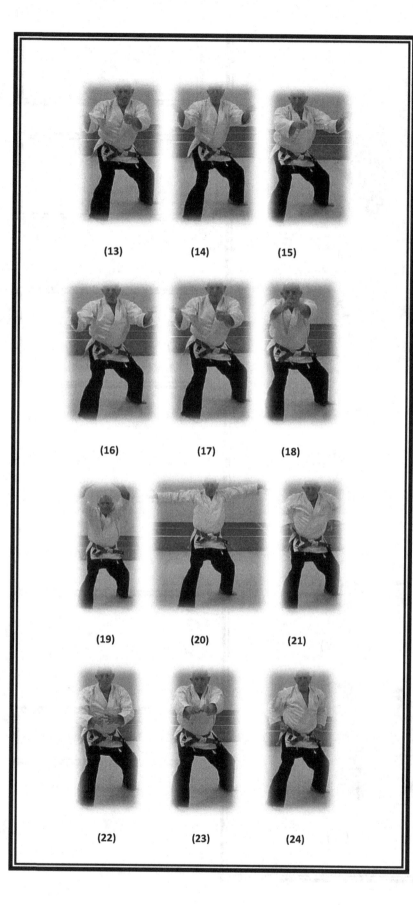

(13) Punch middle left.

(14 Return to Middle block, (Ude-Uki)

(15) Punch middle right.

(16) Return to Middle Block (Ude-Uki.

(17) Punch Middle left.

(18) On this punch bring right hand out, reach up around in big circle, as in Next pictures.

(19) Reaching right up in the Air.

(20) come down around to the hips.

(21) close both hands on hips, then open them again.

(22) From hips double thrused out to centre.

(23) Close hands turn over.

(24) Pull back to hips.

Sanchin Kata

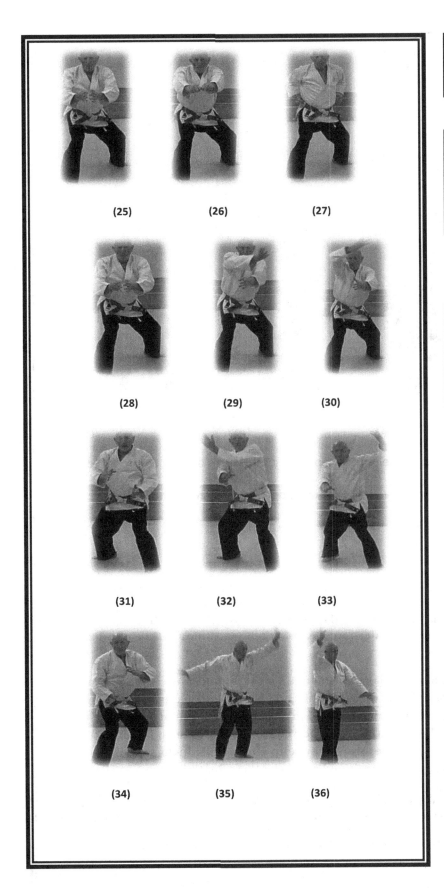

Sanchin Kata

(25) Double Spear hands.

(26) Close fist turn over pull back.

(27) Pull back to hips keeping elbows close to hips.

(28) Double Spear hands.

(29) Parry to your Left, Left hand.

(30) Hand goes over head to the right, then step back,

(31) Left hand then goes around in a circle over your head, to top of right hand, making an energy ball.

(32) Parry to left, left hand.

(33) Hand goes over head to the left, then step back.

(34) Right hand then goes around in a circle over your head, to top of left hand making an energy ball.

(35) Left hand raises' in the air followed with the right in a large circle.

(36) Raised right hand high above your head, ready to strike d

On finishing
Sanchin Kata

(37)   (38)   (39)   (40)

(37) Right hand into left palm, right heel into left in step. (38) Hand's by side feet together (yoi)

(39) Feet together Bow. (40) Feet shoulder wide (Hachi Dachi).

Tensho & sanchin kata's and

The different principles of chi- Kung breathing.

Combining Chi-Kung breathing with Kata's and the way we practice them in Shoto's traditional Karate Kai. The mechanism of the Tencho and Sanchin kata's are a little different, in that there is dynamic tension used, and the principles that Mr. Charles Atlas practiced many years ago. Mr Charles atlas used the principle of contracting the muscle against muscle, using tension, which will help to build your muscles, and give you strength.

For much of the 20th century Charles Atlas was America's most famous muscle man. Atlas emigrated from Italy as a boy, and in his teens he built up his physique using a system of bodybuilding which he later dubbed 'Dynamic Tension'. Atlas advertisements appeared in comic books and magazines and made Atlas into a pop culture icon; his most famous ad, a cartoon in which a scrawny young man resolves to bulk up after a bully kicks sand in his face, ran for years. It was a great success and continued on after Atlas's death in 1972.

Tencho and Sanchin uses this very same principle, producing strength, because of the muscle against muscle principle. Each move in the form is using all your muscles at once, legs, arms, stomach, the under arms as well as the wrists, and forearms. Used with Chi-kung breathing as applied in Tai-Chi, this will give all-round exercise for developing every muscle and cell in your body inducing this strength.

As I explained, these forms are different from the way we normally practice are Kata's. But if you understand why we practice the two kata's Tencho and Sanchin the way they are done, then you will understand the vital forms for the special breathing method. The Sanchin Kata must be done very slowly with great power and when breathing in silently and slowly, as the hands are coming towards you then excelling your breath quite loudly as your hands are going away from you.

In both of these kata's, the Sanchin stance (Hour glass stances) is employed throughout, which is done under a strong tension of upper body and legs being pushed and pulled in a dynamic way, as I explained of the same principles' of Mr Charles Atlas. You can develop and attain greater bodily strength particularly to a powerful Diaphragm with the dynamic tension of your Kata Movements.

On using the tension around and under the arms and the Diaphragm as you move through the movements of the Kata, bracing your legs and thighs, turning your feet inwards, as in the stance of Sanchin Dachi, (hour glass) stance, pushing in and pushing out, at the same time using this dynamic-tension. By applying these movements in this way, the body muscles are being developed just the same way as a weight lifter will induce lifting weights. A weight lifter will breathe out as he lifts, as in the same way you are breathing out as you move through the form, tensing your muscles as you do so.

In Sanchin emphasis is on the double Udi-Uke, and the emphasises on middle thrust punch, 'where as', the Tensho Kata uses the open hand much more like Tai-Chi and Kung-Fu movements of Wing-Chun, the palm and heel strikes and the twisting of the wrists are used. Some people will use dumbbells in their hands to assist as they practice.

Although our main Kata's remain relaxed and flowing without this tension, which induces relaxation. To meditate and just be able to concentrate on your breathing, the sitting position is another way, (Sei-Za) or (Tai-Za).

'Sensei Robert Huntley',

using the Dynamic tension principle, in The Sanchin Kata.
This is a good example of hard work and dedication as;
at the time of this picture being taken Sensei Huntley was fifty five years old.

Chapter (18).   # The advantage of mixed

Training programs and disciplines.

In my experience of developing training programs for courses or club training, the benefits are clear.

Those that adopted a wider view of learning see greater results in both the individual and club members as a team. The traditional view of learning martial arts from only one organization and keeping blinker on from other ideals can be /narrow-minded.

Those that adopt a wider view of learning see greater results from all the disciplines, Ju-Jitsu, Karate, Karate-Ju-Jitsu, Tai Chi, Aikido, and Judo, ECT.

The result can be dramatic, instilling within your main art, all the good points you can find from other Groups, where all the arts are together under one roof. Nevertheless, your traditional roots of relevant classroom based basics are still so important, Remaining focused on your main style.

If you facilitate a discussion-training group, you can meet the needs of your organization by adopting training programs to suit the individual learning process, and on sessions where you meet for training on a mixed discipline basis, you can deliver key principle learning points of your main discipline.

To be able to give impact through your structural training of your group, you have to deliver stimulating sessions that are informative and interesting to keep their attention to be able to show the core of your competence of training, so as they can see that a wider evaluation of your discipline would be of interest to learn.

When teaching on these shorter courses it is also important to give a very good demonstration of your techniques, delivering a good beginning, middle, and a good end to the session.

Having an understanding of each discipline is one-step towards building a better understanding of techniques. Regular Master classes cannot be a bad thing to presenting their specialist subjects.

Fully explore the benefits of an integrated approach to learning; these courses however highlight some key points for consideration, implementing simple learning.

All systems joining a Malty styled group transform one or more inputs to outputs using resources within that group to identify their techniques for all. Malty styled groups who approach to developing this greater understanding, is to view your group as a system.

Developing this common understanding has shown to have significant results in improving all relationships and communication between all parties.

In addition, any new and experienced trainers from any discipline's and individuals who called upon to deliver training as part of a wider visualization to what the styled group are all about. These groups should be known to have a very high standard and be already vetted, and if you are an instructor looking to join an association like no other, which puts the students needs first that do not interfere, dictates, or demand, in how your club or clubs run. You are most welcome to apply for an Instructors training pack within Shoto's Traditional Karate Kai. These are the key points of courses overview, benefits of harnessing the full potential of a training group.

Facilitating-discussion; participation; Analyzing; Evaluation; Motivation and Feedback.

Chapter (19)

Student's progress:

When a new student fills in the heath declaration, and you find he has some form of ailment, but which it do's not stop him/her training. (I.E Epilepsy, Asthma, M.E. ECT ;)
It is still your responsibility to find out, and understand that person's disability or ailment from any medical ancillary practitioner, nurse, or books, in the diagnosis treatment and the management of that student's medical and psychological problems, and what to watch for if a crisis happens, and to assist in their training programs.

With a new student in mind, every aspect should be considered and then planed. You should pay Particular attention of a new student for their integration.

Individual training tailored for students with one to one intuition, structured to ensure that each student makes the most of the available experience of techniques on a daily basis.

Instruction between instructors and students should have post implementation of their techniques to ensuring your student is continuing to meet all your criteria and key objectives in accordance with ever changing needs to obtain the next level in his/her grading syllabus.

Trying to give students self-esteem, in addition, to build and strengthen self-esteem, and respect in your-self, and your student, to help achieve their personal goals, the grading syllabus is the main facture to setting these goals.

The relationship between self-esteem and self-respect self-confidence and self-motivation, which is to be considered when helping them achieve these goals.

As she/he reaches these goals, this will bring their self-esteem up, and give them discipline turning aggression and submission into assertiveness and self-discipline and attitude for the better.

In your teaching set your presentation with confidence and with an exciting and professional manner. Use your body language to maximize your presentation. Handle nerves by channelling your nervous energy into your presentation.

This communication between instructor and student will influence in achieving objectives within martial arts the main goals and potentials in developing their group. Never underestimate the importance of loyalty and their morale.

A change in programs has to be clear to all instructors. If you do not know where you are going, how do you expect to get there?

It is important to make changes clear, so as not too interrupted or impedes a student's progress.   Goals are set so that the student's enthusiasm will not diminish.

For organizations, which manage changes skilfully, become a driving force that perpetuates successes in improving techniques in, Kata's, Kimute, Sampon Kimute and all practices to do with that organization, hopefully to evolve the structure of that group.

Sensei Griffiths presented Kirsty Cratchley & Tony Williams with their 1ˢᵗ Dan Black belts. Tony with Sensei Robert Huntley 5ᵗʰ Dan

This is a picture of a young Rolf Whitman, and a close friend of my Son Graham, who trained at our club for Karate, and also trains at Ju-Do. Here he is winning a top award in competition in Ju-Do at Gloucester 1976.

Always recognize the difference in teaching children from adults. Studying the child protection policy as lay down by Shotos-traditional-Karate-Kai working with children, all instructors should avoid at all times any terms or gesture, behaviour, or contact with a child that could be misinterpreted as abuse.

I recommend that all instructors should, 'see that parents are to be present while a child is training', where a child is under the age of sixteen. It is the instructor's responsibility to ensure the safety, and welfare of a small person at all times in their care.

Do not allow any person of a criminal character especially if it is some sort of child abuse to train within your club, especially not evolved in couching.

Sensei Griffiths teaching young children at

Seminar Stoke on Trent 2004

Every child and young person, who participates in martial arts, should be able to practice and participate in an enjoyable and safe environment, and to be protected from abuse. You are to protect them from physical, sexual, and or emotional harm, neglect, or bullying. Very clear procedures and practices will ensure everyone knows and understands exactly what is expected of them in relation to the protection of children and young people within your group, sport, or way of life.

Me in our Gym at the Rea Bridge House, 1980.

With my Son Graham, around the age of 12,

My Son Graham started training from the age of six, he used to watch me training, and wanted to do it off his own bat, and he was never forced into it and took to it like a duck to water. In this picture he was a Brown Belt and ready to take his Black Belt. I am very proud of him and he trained just like an adult. Being my son I use to push him very hard looking back perhaps too much, I did not want it to look like favouritism because he was my son. So really my Son had it harder than most Students, and by him still training and doing his best had proved he was worthy of any Black Belt a man could earn.

He is now a grown man and has Children of his own a Girl and a Boy Larrisa and Brandon, of which they started training as well.

117

This is Graham Griffiths my son doing a leg sweep on Dean George
At are gym in the garden at Rea Bridge, 1981

Sensei, James Merritt's club in Tony Pandy in Wales, Sensei Griffiths and Sensei Robert Huntley, sitting in the foreground, centre. Sensei Merritt on the right and two of my members at the back centre, next to Rob Notley, Tony Williams and Phil Knickenberg, 2009 on the left Douglas Cochran.

I would like to say; Sensei James Merritt's club is so very outstanding, which is accredited to him and Brian Morse. The club has been going strong for many long years, and the first instructor that I met who was the founder of the club 'was Brian'; I first met Brian about 25 years ago when he invited me to teach at his club.

I will always have the deepest respect for both these instructors; they have given so much to the Martial arts. They have helped in giving kids a good start in life through this discipline of the art.

I was invited to an evening do, in 2009 to help to give outstanding achievements awards to his pupils throughout the year of 2009, and I was so impressed with the attendants of the pupils and parents that turned up. It was an amazing evening as I got to meet past and present members, where ex pupils had brought their children along to practice. Incidentally James Merritt was a young pupil of Brian's when he was about only ten years old and now he is helping running the club as club instructor; he is in this photo which was taken quite a few years ago.

James Merritt on my left, around ten years old, he is now married and has a child of his own.

James Merritt receaving his 3rd Dan from Sensei Griffiths, which was well deserved.

Rob Notley on the receaving end of a back hander, by Morgann Bryce Cochran. Sensei Griffiths with Rob Notley, at Christmas achievement awards evening 2010. Rob now helps with the running of the club'.

Sensei Griffiths & Sensei Brian Morse after a photo shoot on Stinchcome hill, 1980.

Back row left to right David Pincott, Sensei Brian Morse, Sensei Douglas Cochran, Sensei Rob Notley,

Front row, Erin Davey, Courtney Ann Cochran, Morgann Bryce Cochran.

Sensei Gerald Griffiths, Tai-Chi Single Whip, On Maslin Beach, South Australia.

Chapter (20). Your health and what you should be looking for in your practice

Doing sport, and keeping fit, helps to keep your immune system in good condition, which helps flush out toxins, and helps fight bugs, even slow exercise like Tai Chi can help.

The martial arts can raise immunity according to studies, our poor old joints can take a right battering throughout our lives, so it is not very surprising that the older we get the more chance we are likely to experience arthritis, or aching bones and stiff joints. Painkillers and anti-inflammatory drugs do help, but more than often, they have side effects. Some people use copper. Cells in the body utilises copper together with iron and zinc the trio complements of these minerals are essential to our well being. In China, the Chinese maintain that through Tai Chi and exercise, the human body is built up of three major essentials. The 'yi' (mind), 'Qi' (energy) and 'Jing' (hormones), by nurturing and with practice will help to prolong your life, if by dissipating them you could die young. By Qigong, breathing exercising you can preserve these essentials. The 'Yi', you will enjoy the state of relaxation and tranquillity. The promotion of blood circulation is increased by 'Qi' exercises, which expands your vital capacity of blood circulation. The physical vitality of your body's internal balance can be induced through the exercises of 'Jing'. All of these things come from the deep concentration of practice, in all the benefits of exercising the functions of the central nervous system. As you move through the Tai chi exercise, you train the body and mind at the same time, you stimulate with the slow movements, the cerebral cortex enabling you to relax, and relieve the cerebral cortex of pathological excitation, which may be the causes of your ailments of your nervous and mental disorders and diseases, thus giving you better health.

With the elasticity of your lung tissues increasing, your lungs capacitating to various nerves of the vogues nerves, will ensure adequate supplies of blood and oxygen to the tissues of your cardiovascular respiratory system?

Helping to the retarding of the ossification of your rib's cartilages and ventilation capacity of the lungs improving the exchange of oxygen and carbon dioxide and end results are, a stronger diaphragm.

By trying that much harder in getting lower in your stances during your slow movements, you will strengthen your legs muscles, in your calves, thighs, and joints. Hinged movements that are in the waist will in turn strengthen the spine, the lumbar, and vertebra of the spinal column. 'Not forgetting a good posture'.

Sensei Robert Huntley doing a side kick in the gym at the Rea Bridge

Health and safety in the Do-Jo

Which is important fitness, or 'Karate' (Tai-Chi)? 'Well Quality is fitness for purpose'.

What is a safe system in the Do-Jo and the benefits to belong to an organization that puts its students first, looking after their safety during and after practice, 'these are obvious'.

The properly implemented programme of risk assessments can assist in the prevention of injuries ECT! With-in the Do-Jo. Where there is physical training there is always an element of risk to injury or accidents.

If the instructors (coaches) are aware of these risks and is completely on 'his', 'her' guard to eliminate these risks. This makes a better place to train.

Recognise the differences in teaching children from adults. Studying the child protection policy as laid down by the Shotos-Traditional-Karate-Kai. Apart from the corporate and personal benefits arising from risk assessment, instructors and students have a duty to make sure the areas are safe. When practice has started responsibility for the floors to be swept and clean, 'no sharp objects on the floor'. Assessment of the risks to health and safety of other students, and the risk assessment; principles and practices is designed for everyone;   'keep risks down'.

Muscle spasms are caused by tension and stress, strains, and sprains, from working unused muscles occurs quite often, so it's so important to start training at a steady pace, building gradually to awaken these muscles, to build strength to help support the back (vertebrae). Most important do not over do it.

From the beginning always warm-up slowly and safely, and know your own limitations.

Your Back is important treat it with care, ligaments connects the vertebrae, and between the vertebrae are soft discs that cushion and protect the bones.

Nerves run through the spine and go to the rest of the body. In fact it supports your whole body. The spinal column is S-shaped and the stack of vertebrae bones literally hold you up.

Your back is supported by muscles that run along the spinal column, working closely with the muscles in your stomach. Being overweight especially if you have a potbelly puts a lot of extra strain on those muscles.

It's even worse if you are out of shape because the muscles get weak and cannot do their job well. Gradual training with good martial arts, Shoto`s Traditional-Karate-Kai will help build these muscles back to their full potential.

Also by not keeping yourself fit, you can be in danger of various muscle strain and hiatus hernia, this is where parts of your stomach pushes' through the diaphragm wall, which is the muscular sheet that separates the lungs and chest from your abdomen. You may not have any symptoms but will often cause pain and some form of heart burn one of the most common of hernia's is where the ring of muscles (the sphincter) that form a valve between the oesophagus and stomach which slides up through the diaphragm. I myself have had a hernia which was in my groan. I had to have an operation

where they cut you open, basically they push it back in then stitch a layer of mesh' over the affected area to strengthen the wall behind the muscles. There are a number of things you can do to help. Change your life style for one, eat smaller meals, but more frequently, avoid bending and lifting heavy objects after a heavy meal.

Chapter (21) Streetwise Preventive self-defence

I have no wish to give you paranoia, but being prepared on the street means thinking ahead.

Looking at what can be done, for safety on going out late at night, ECT:

Violent crimes by strangers in public are still a very small part of violent crime. The chances of you or a member of your family becoming a victim of violence are quite small. You don't have to be making big changes in your life style to make yourself safe.

Making yourself safe; for example from Muggings, robbery, or assault, just a few precautions are all you need, and many are just common sense.

Simple things of going in to a lift, if you don't like the look of the person that goes in before you.

Do not worry about hurting feelings, 'get the next one.

Thinking ahead taking precautions on parking your car during the day light hours is there adequate lighting, for when you come back in the darkness hour.

Rather than park in a dark car park, maybe it would be better parking on a main-lit street.

Keeping to well-lit busy areas when walking:

Try not to walk alone at night; no short cuts over wasteland, keep to well lighting, where the roads have many people, keep away from, dark shrubbery, alleys and doorways.

Try not to let your friend, walk home on their own, when you go out together, go home together.

If you are out jogging don't use the same rout every time, and use bright reflective clothing. Carry a personal attack alarm; you can get them from the police station, or your D.I.Y. store. Wearing a Stereo; you may not be able to hear the traffic or someone coming up behind you.

Try to walk to on facing traffic. Do not wear expensive Jewellery, if you don't need to carry a hand-bag, leave it at home, 'this is a mugger's invitation'. Keep things in your pocket.

If you have to have a hand-bag, try not to put everything in it. Try spreading your valuables in different pockets on your person. Keep your mobile phone hidden, if you're chatting on the phone you won't hear someone coming up behind you. If someone tries to snatch your bag let it go, your safety is much more important than your belongings.

Deserted bus stops are a big no-no, and do not hitch a lift. If you have to use public transport wait at a busy well lit bus stop, sit near the driver on the bus' and if on a train journey avoid falling asleep, keeping your valuables close on your lap.

If a car stops or slows down near you and you are threatened, shout or scream to attract attention to yourself. If you are being followed try crossing the street do it more than once or twice to see if they follow. If still worried go to the nearest place where there are people. Knock on someone's door if necessary, or go to a pub, or a place where there are a lot of people, then call the police. But avoid a phone box as you could be isolated.

Only uses registered Taxis, and try to us the same company, 'book in advance'.

If you are going to be late going home after your evening out, arrange a lift with a friend, or book a taxi. Keep a telephone number of a reliable taxi firm at hand, whenever you can pre-book your Taxi and phone a local firm. When you leave the venue make sure you're getting in the licensed Cab you ordered.

If the car is an old banger, as good as dam it is not a licensed Taxi. If there is no license on display forget it. Your driver should have a Badge on display with the License number showing.

Maybe if the driver asks you for directions he doesn't know the area, and if the driver has bypassed the front of the Queue to pick you up – it's not a coincidence.

(DON'T GET IN)

Try to remember to use the cash machine in the daylight hours before you go out in the evening. Watch for any suspicious characters hanging around near the cash Machine. If in doubt go back later, or look for another machine.

There are warning signs on most machines, if there is something unusual about the machine, where the card go's in, do not use it, you need to report it to the bank, or the police strait away. Be careful with your pin number never write it down and shield your pin number from people as you type it in.

Do not count your money near the machine in full view of strangers. Do not walk around with large amounts of money in your pocket.

Being aware of Drink Spiking

One of the things that can happen today is the spiking of drinks, do not leave your drink on the table unattended when dancing or going to the toilet, get a friend to look after it for you.

You can get these pop bottle locks, which is a good investment. 'And don't let strangers give you a drink'. Drink spiking is often in the news and linked to the rape drug 'Rohypnol'. Drink spiking is when something is added to your drink without your knowledge. This can include additional alcohol as well as drugs of mind altering substances. It is often rare but on the increase, and for your own safety, must be watched out for. Woman can be the main victims of drink spiking, but there are and can be up to 11% of males

It may be a bit of fun to some but in the law's eyes, can lead to 10 years imprisonment and these penalties' can be much higher if sexual assault, robbery or thefts has taken place.

If you are with a group of people, do not go off with anyone without telling your friends where you are going, and go only with preferably someone you know.

When you arrive home, keep your keys handy for when you reach your front door, you do not want to be scrabble-ling around in a bag.

Driving to and from Shift work is usually late at night, so always lock your car, check the back seat when you get in, see if no one has broken in, when driving keep windows closed and doors locked, keep all belongings of value out of sight, preferably in the boot. Carry a small torch in the car.

'Be streetwise & be safe'.

Crime safety, at your door.

People need to be secure from crime; most of crime is done on property more than people. So you need to make your home a secure place. Hopefully my writings will help reduce the risk of being a victim. You can start by being safer and protected by securing you home. You can do this for yourself and your family and belongings, by following some of the suggestions I have advised.

Crimes sometimes are just a spur of the moment, like the invitation of an open window, or your valuables on display in your home or car. Most of these suggestions are common sense. But will make a difference,

On going out double   check you've locked the door, close all your windows even if you are going out for a short time. On old sash windows it will help to but modern locks on, and you can buy most of these from Diy stores.

Burglars don't like to smash windows they make too much noise and can catch people's attention. If you have deadlocks on your doors and at night make it hard for thief's to get in and out. And don't leave the keys near the door, keep garage and car keys out of sight.

Most visitors at the door are genuine, but some people that turn up at your door may be undesirables to trick you out of your belongings. Sometimes they are in two's and known as distraction burglars these bogus callers will distract you while his accomplice will steal your money and valuables.

These bogus callers are usually well dress and look like officials, they may even have ID cards and claim to be a policeman or from the council, gas, water and electricity companies. If you are not expecting anyone from any of these companies don't let them in. they can be very convincing and persuasive, and if they say for you to ring there companies number, do not use their card, ring the number from your own telephone directory. Checking if the number is the same as the caller, While you are checking them out, always keep the chain lock on your door, keep your back doors locked, not forgetting to take the key out and not on show.

If you are expecting someone, and this official visitor has arranged an appointment with you beforehand, check there ID carefully against the letter, the company has sent you, Is the name the same on their ID card as the one in your official letter, do they look the same as their ID card.

 There may be a password that you have already agreed on, if the caller does not know it, check and double check that the caller is genuine, any doubts what so ever don't let them in.

If they are genuine they will not mind waiting.

Watch out for bogus builders and repair men tricking you into unnecessary work never agree to have work done. If you think you have or need work to be done go to replicable companies and get two or three quotes. You can find these companies by your local councils trading standards office.

If you are having trouble from anyone you think is a bogus person, weather it is a builder or so called officials. Then report it to the police dial 999 and tell them what has happened. Try to remember what that person looked like and give a description to the police. If you have a kind neighbour or caretaker or neighbourhoods watch tell them as well, so if they target others in your neighbourhood people will be on their guard.

 The earlier the police and everybody know that bogus callers are working in the area, the quicker the authorities can investigate and catch them. Warning only put your chain lock on when you answer the door, in case you have to get out in an emergency

Chapter (22)

Grading Syllabus

Shoto's Traditional Karate Kai.

Regulation on promotion of Dan Grade's and Title's.

1sr Dan, Those persons that have passed their examination on finishing the courses & grades as set by the group.

3 years from a novice to first Dan Black Belt. Must be over 16 years old for Dan Grade. Under 16, junior Black belt. Must retake examination after 16 years old.

2nd Dan same as above, Not less than 2 years after promotion to 1st Dan.

3rd Dan same as above not less than 3 years promotion to 2nd Dan.

4th Dan same as above, not less than 4 years after 3rd Dan.

Renshi. People who have passed the exam that are able to teach the required practical Grading syllabus (A disciplined Teacher) not less than 2 years after promotion to 4th Dan.

6th Dan. those that have passed their exam and are able to teach the required practical grading syllabus & of good character... Not less than 4 years after promotion to 5th Dan.

Kyoshi. Same as above. Those that acquired the spirit of the Martial arts & practice of Shoto's Traditional Karate Kai. (One who acquired the true Buda spirit)?

7th Dan. same as above. Not less than 2 years after receiving the title of Kyoshi.

Two signatures to signify that this grading syllabus is the true example of the principle of; The Shoto's Traditional Karate Kai.

Sensei_____

Sign_____

Sensei_____

Sign_____

1st Dan (Black belt).

(Renchi), Excellence can be granted at time of promotion to 4th Dan. & (Kyoshi), at time of 6th Dan. At the Discretion of the committee; (Note), Time served, the overall ability may be a factor in the assessment of a candidate to reducing the periods stipulated in this timetable. Comparisons to the other Yadansha already at any given grade may also be used for an assessment, under the complete discretion of the Examiners that are assessing, and where the Committee deems to be acceptable.

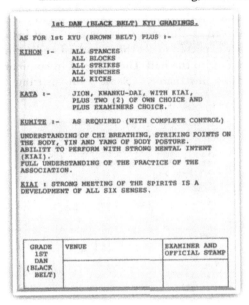

The Bo and Bokken must be practiced by all brown and black belts.

First Dan Black Belt every body's goal, but this is the start.
Grading Syllabus; and Kata's

A record of grades to give the student some idea of what is expected of him, her, I.E. Dedication to practice, attendance, attitude, personal development. ECT; A student will be required to be graded to a physical of proficiency relative to their grade.

Grading will be on the following basis ==: Note: = Automatic grading can be awarded by the chief instructor at any time, at his own discretion on approved association courses.

Character. = Attitude. = Perfection, of stances. = Basic blocks, and kicks. Practice of the Kata form's as presented by Chief Instructor (Sensei). The knowledge and appreciation of techniques. Development of control, speed, Power, precision and form.

Teaching ability and assistance given to others. Searching, and understanding of circular movements of the hips, and breathing. Forward & back stances, in posture (Yin/yang). Positive Mental intent when performing all techniques.

Time Practised: = From 6th Kyu to 2nd kyu: = ---------------- 3 Months between grades. From 2nd Kyu to 1st kyu : = --------------- 6 months between grades. Courses must be attended as regularly as possible and club practice must be on a regular basis. Club instructors will keep a record of this. 1st kyu brown belts must wait 12 months practice before taking a Dan grade, and must attend at least three courses in that year and have them recorded in the grading book by club or course instructor.

Students failing 1st kyu brown belt must wait 4 months before re-grading. Students failing Dan grade must wait 6 months. Red tabs must be worn on belts until students have past 6th Kyu. Yellow belts must have white tabs until full yellow. White tabs must be worn on brown belts 1st & 2ndlevel brown until full Brown Membership must be renewed whether grading or not. Checks will be carried out on courses. Club instructors will be held responsible for this. Students under 16 years of age will be classified as juniors and will be graded as such. Students becoming 16 years of age will go from junior to senior. But will be re-assessed during transition by chief instructors, and be issued with their book stamped up to date. Strict self-discipline and proper Karate Etiquette must be observed at all times towards the Chief instructor. Club instructors, and senior brown belts and black belt are expected to set this standard and maintain it at all times. Bowing on entering the hall. After warm up, Bow to the hall. Then second in command will call compliment to Sensei. Then bow to club instructor. 'Same for sitting Bow'.

GRADINGS / TRAINING. ALL STUDENTS WILL BE EXPECTED TO REACH A STANDARD OF ABILITY AT DIFFERENT LEVELS OF PRACTICE OF THE FOLLOWING :-

STANCES

ZENKUTSU DACHI	- FORWARD FRONT LEG STANCE
KIBA DACHI	- STRADDLE HORSE RIDING STANCE
KOKUTSU DACHI	- BACK LEG STANCE
SANCHIN	- HOUR GLASS LEG STANCE
NEKO ASHI	- CAT LEG STANCE
TSURU ASHI	- CRANE LEG STANCE
HANGETSU	- HALF MOON LEG STANCE
TEIJI	- T LEG STANCE
HACHIJI	- NATURAL STANCE

BLOCKS

GEDAN BARAI	- DOWNWARD SWEEPING BLOCK
JODAN AGE UKE	- UPPER LEVEL BLOCK
UDE UKE	- ARM BLOCK
UCHI UKE	- INSIDE BLOCK
TEISHO BARAI	- PALM HEEL BLOCK
MOROTE UKE	- REINFORCED FOREARM BLOCK
SHOTO BARAI	- SWORD ARM BLOCK

STRIKES

UCHI	- STRIKE
NUKITE	- SPEAR HAND (FINGERS CLOSED)
NAITO UCHI	- RIDGE HAND STRIKE
TEISHO UCHI	- PALM HAND STRIKE
EMPI UCHI	- ELBOW STRIKE
SHOTO UCHI	- SWORD HAND STRIKE

PUNCHES

OI TSUKI	- LUNGE STEP PUNCH
SEIKEN TSUKI	- FORE FIST PUNCH
GYAKU TSUKI	- REVERSE PUNCH
MOROTE TSUKI	- DOUBLE FIST PUNCH
MAWASHI TSUKI	- ROUND HOUSE PUNCH
TETTSUI	- HAMMER FIST
IPPONKEN	- FORE KNUCKLE FIST

KICKS

MAE GERI	- FRONT KICK
FUMIKOMI	- STAMPING KICK
YOKO KE KOMI GERI	- SIDE KICK (EDGE OF FOOT)
MAWASHI GERI	- ROUND HOUSE KICK
USHIRO GERI	- BACK KICK (HEEL)
MIKAZUKI GERI	- CRESCENT KICK
TOBI GERI	- JUMP KICK
MAE TOBI GERI	- JUMPING FRONT KICK
YOKO TOBI GERI	- JUMPING SIDE KICK
MAWASHI TOBI GERI	- JUMPING ROUND HOUSE KICK
MIKAZUKI TOBI GERI-	JUMPING CRESCENT KICK
ASHI BARAI	- FOOT SWEEP
HIZI GERI	- KNEE STRIKE
NAMI GAESHI	- RETURNING WAVE DEFLECTING KICK

KATA'S

KATA'S OF THE ASSOCIATION :-
TAIKYOKO:SHODAN;NIDAN;SANDAN
HEIAN:SHODAN;NIDAN;SANDAN;YODAN;GODAN
TEKKI:SHODAN;NIDAN;SANDAN
BASSAI-DAI, BASSAI-SHO, KWANKU-DAI, KWANKU-SHO,
HANGETSU, SANCHIN, TENSAO, EMPI, MAKHO, GANKAKU,
JION, JIAN, JUTTE, NEID-SHO, TAI-CHI, LONG - YANG,
BO KATA'S.

KYU GRADINGS

6th KYU - (WHITE BELTS)

KIHON :-

ZENKUTSU DACHI	-	GEDEN BARAI
ZENKUTSU DACHI	-	OI ZUKI MOVING FORWARD
ZENKUTSU DACHI	-	MAE GERI

KATA'S :-

TAIKYOKU SHODAN
TAIKYOKU NIDAN WITH KIAI (MEETING OF THE SPIRITS)
TAIKYOKU SANDAN

STANCES :-

AN UNDERSTANDING OF THE FOLLOWING DIFFERENT
STANCES :-
KIBA DACHI
ZENKUTSU DACHI - AND SHOW THE DIFFERENCE
KOKUTSU DACHI
UNDERSTANDING TURNING IN ZENKUTSU DACHI
BOW-REI (STANDING)

6th KYU MUST BE ABLE TO PRACTICE EVERYTHING ON
THIS PAGE AND WITH 8 SESSIONS OF PRACTICE BE ABLE
TO TAKE THIS GRADE, 'CLUB INSTRUCTORS DISCRETION'.

GRADE	VENUE	EXAMINER AND OFFICIAL STAMP
6th KYU		

KYU GRADINGS

5th KYU (YELLOW BELTS 1st AND 2nd LEVEL)

AS FOR 6th KYU (WHITE BELT) PLUS :-

KIHON :-

BLOCKS	-	JODAN AGE UKE
		TAISHO BARAI
		ICHI KOMI
PUNCHES	-	OI ZUKI (CHUDAN/JODAN LEVELS)
		GYAKU ZUKI
KICKS	-	FUMIKOMI
		KE KOMI
TEN NO KATA	-	STEPPING FORWARD, ZENKUTSU WITH KNOWN BLOCK, AND GYAKU ZUKI
KATA'S :-		HEIAN SHODAN WITH KIAI

SITTING CORRECTLY (SIEZA / ZAZAN)
BOW - REI SITTING

GRADE	VENUE	EXAMINER AND OFFICIAL STAMP
5th KYU		

KYU GRADINGS

1st KYU (BROWN BELT)

AS FOR 2nd KYU (BLUE BELT) PLUS :-

THERE ARE TWO LEVELS OF 1st KYU. YOUR ABILITY TO PERFORM THE TECHNIQUES DECIDES WHICH LEVEL OF 1st KYU YOU ARE AWARDED: BROWN BELT (WHITE TAB) AND OR FULL BROWN.

KIHON :-
```
STANCES   -  ALL STANCES
PUNCHES   -  ALL PUNCHES
STRIKES   -  ALL STRIKES
KICKS     -  ALL KICKS PRACTISED
KARATE    -  COMBINATIONS AS REQUIRED
KUMITE    -  AS REQUIRED
```

KATA'S :- HEIAN GODAN, BASSAI-DAI, TEKKI NIDAN, HANGETSU WITH KIAI
PLUS KATA OF YOUR OWN CHOICE AND PLUS EXAMINERS CHOICE

COMPLETE TWO MAN FIGHTING SET.

TO BE ABLE TO PRACTICE WITH BO AND BOKKEN.

AN UNDERSTANDING OF THE USE OF HIP WIND UP.

GRADE	VENUE	EXAMINER AND OFFICIAL STAMP
1st KYU		

KYU GRADINGS

2nd KYU (BLUE BELT)

AS FOR 3rd KYU (GREEN BELT) PLUS :-

KIHON :-

BLOCKS   - ALL BLOCKS STEPPING FORWARD/BACK

PUNCHES   - MAWASHI ZUKI (ROUND HOUSE PUNCH)

STANCE   - FUDO DASHI

KICKS   - USHIRO GERI (BACK KICK)

STRIKES   - EMPI UCHI (ELBOW STRIKE)
             TEISHO UCHI (PALM HEEL STRIKE)
             TO BE SHOWN DURING SANBON KUMITE

KATA :-
HEIAN GODAN, TEKKI SHODAN WITH KIAI

KUMITE :-
SANBON KUMITE - TWO MAN FIGHTING SET UP TO TEKKI KATA

UNDERSTANDING OF DISTANCE, TIMING, HARMONY WITH A PARTNER.
UNDERSTANDING OF BREATHING, USE OF HIPS AND CIRCULAR MOVEMENTS

GRADE	VENUE	EXAMINER AND OFFICIAL STAMP
2nd KYU		

KYU GRADINGS

3rd KYU (GREEN BELT)

AS FOR 4th KYU (ORANGE BELT) PLUS :-

KIHON :-

BLOCKS   - ALL BLOCKS STEPPING FORWARD/BACK

STRIKES - SHOTO UCHI (SWORD HAND STRIKE)

PUNCH   - MAI TE (LEADING ARM PUNCH)

KICKS   - ASHI BARAI (FOOT SWEEP)
            MAWASHI GERI (ROUND HOUSE KICK)
            MAE TOBI GERI (JUMPING FRONT KICK)

AN UNDERSTANDING OF THE DIFFERENCE BETWEEN SNAP AND THRUST KICKS (KEACE - KI KOME)

KATA'S :-

HEIAN SANDAN WITH KAI
HEIAN YODAN
TWO MAN FIGHTING SET UP TO SANDAN KATA

TEN NO KATA :-

STEPPING FORWARD/STEPPING BACKWARD/TURNING

UNDERSTANDING OF ICK A TIA WITH THE ARMS

GRADE	VENUE	EXAMINER AND OFFICIAL STAMP
3rd KYU		

KYU GRADINGS

4th KYU (ORANGE BELT)

AS FOR 5th KYU (YELLOW BELT) PLUS :-

KIHON :-

BLOCKS   - SHOTO UKE
            UCHI UKE

STRIKES - URAKEN (BACK FIST)
            NUKITE (SPEAR HAND)

KICKS   - MIKAZUKI GERI (CRESCENT KICK)

STANCE   - SANCHIN

BASIC KUMITE (IPPON) STEPPING FORWARD/TURNING/REME

KATA'S :-

HEIAN NIDAN WITH KIAI
SANCHIN

KARATE TWO MAN FIGHTING SET UPTO HEIAN NIDAN KATA

BASIC WORDS OF COMMAND IN THE DOJO BY THE INSTRUCTOR

GRADE	VENUE	EXAMINER AND OFFICIAL STAMP
4th KYU		

Chapter (23)

TAI-CHI

CHI KUNG BREATHING

A Holistic approach to my practice.

I have been practising Tai Chi for a very long time, and still feel that I am only scratching the surface in finding more moves and building my inner strength. I became an instructor and a teacher not just for the physical side but also the mental strength Tai Chi brings out in me, which gives me a positive outlook that fills me with confidence. This is why the enjoyment of practise has stayed with me all this time, and of being able to bring on a student and see their progress as they improve the physical side, and the mental strength they achieve.

Training in Karate and Tai-Chi more so my Tai-Chi I am convinced that the Chi energy which I have experienced in my Tai Chi and Chi Kung, has given me immense complete physical wellbeing and fullness. With this tingling sensation I have experience throughout my circulation and the energy in my palms and fingertips, after the end of a practice. I am sure that with a positive mind this energy can be transmitted into the healing process for me or others.

Acupuncturists, shiatsu, or reiki practitioners are carefully trained to understand the laws of nature to diagnose and acknowledge what therapeutic effectiveness is called for to cure the factor of the disease or ailment to assist the continued flow of Chi energy.

To complement the patient a unique rap-pore is established between practitioner and patients.

With forty years of dedicated practice in Martial Arts. Taking my mind and body over and beyond the average mans capability. Finding that bit extra to push my energy and focused mind of concentration to practice. Giving, and receiving pushing out my concentrated chi energy. Karate, Sampon kumiti, ipon kumiti, Kata, tai Chi, and Qigong are a good argument to giving my opinion to the effects of the Chi energy and feelings within the body.

Sensei Griffiths practicing Tai Chi in his Dojo.

The neuro'chemicals that relieves pain is stimulated with pressure; needles or heat triggers their releasing of your endorphins. By relieving pain you are closing the 'gate'. The gate being the path at which the pain takes to go to the brain. When this is blocked, the muscle relaxes in the damaged area and promotes healing. When relaxed the blood and oxygen is increased to the infected area, thus the blockage of your Chi flow is released and allowed to continue unhindered.

The well being within the body is where your mind and soul is flourishing with environmental harmonious relationships with society and nature. This is your personal Chi. All things are held in Yin & carry Yang, and they are held together in Chi of teaming energy (Translated Man-ho Kwok et al, 1992). The Chinese overview of Chi is its representation of all things. (Air the breath of life and vitality)

'Bioelectrical', 'Electrical energy', 'micro energy', 'radio waves'.

Qi-gong has been practiced in China for thousands of years to prevent illness and to cure illnesses, People, who train in Martial arts, also practice Qi-gong breathing to make them stronger and lethal with their hands and feet. The main principle rests on exchanging the Chi in the body with chi in the Universe.

ELECTRICITY

In this picture of the Rea Bridge outside my Home, You can almost feel the Chi energy coming out of the picture.

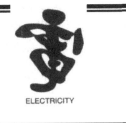

ELECTRICITY

Bio electoral rhythms 'electrical energy, 'micro energy', 'radio waves'. to put a label on it ECT; This creates and maintains all living forms. The Yin and Yang are the two aspects of that energy. Yin and Yang are always present together, they represent the nature of all events and situations, and one cannot separate one from the other.

Energy, (Chi, Chinese); (Ki, Japanese); (Prana, India); (Manna, primal religions); Ha (Hawaiian)

This Hawaiian term of energy I have recently understood is very fascinating as the visitors to the islands find when they visit. They are presented with a wreath of flowers.

The Hawaiian word for breath is Ha, when people are presented with these wreaths; they are greeted with the words Aloha that is an expression of love. The Ha being the breath of life. A healer in Hawaii is known as Kahuna, or the 'masters of breath'.

Chi Meridian lines; With the use of sensitive electrical devices Western scientist have been able to map out and prove the existence of the systems body points of the meridian lines and special pathways that the Chinese call Chi. The Japanese call Ki.

This is the human energy that makes us alive and well, when flowing correctly throughout these meridian lines, high electrical conductivity at the skins surface conducts the body energy most effectively.

This was a picture taken at the bottom of my Garden.

The most fundamental part of our universe is energy. Energy is used to light our towns and cities, and to do work, our vehicles, planes, and trains, and rockets.

All our energy warms our homes, cooks our food, music, and television.
Energy on our farms, power machinery, and tractors. The machinery in our factories is also using energy. The sun gives us light and warm energy. It dries our cloths on a clothes line. Helps plants to grow. Energy is in plants, and is eaten giving energy to people and animals alike, burning food transforming food into energy.

Every-thing we do is connected to energy in one form or another. Moving something, lifting something, heating something, and lighting.
These things are some of the various types of energy. There are many more sources of energy Most of these sources we are fully brought up on and can simplify and understand them.
These being;
. Transportation energy. . Wind energy.   . Solar (Sun energy). Nuclear energy.   . Hydropower, ocean energy. . The natural gas, fossil fuels-coal and oil. . Biomass energy – energy from trees and plants.
. Electricity energy.

Chi Energy and more

All the energy I have written about is all to do with and conducive to Chi energy. This is in all things within the whole universe ECT; **and more**

I will write about, and try to give you an insight of this energy from the evidence I have gathered and experienced through the practice of martial arts.

The chi energy how the Chinese perceive it, and are convinced that Chi is not just a postulate, but is a vital energy which is experienced through the disciplines such as Chi-Kung breathing Tai-Chi, Kung-Fu, Shiatsu & acupuncture, and Karate ECT; and more.

The word Chi is a Chinese word for energy in English, Ki (Japanese), Mana (Primal religions) Ha (Hawaii). And many more words for energy in many other cultures.

Prior to the commencement of Chi Kung breathing, or your Tai-Chi form, / Kata.

Do what I call a dry wash; some say an energy fix or quick fix. Stimulating the body's surface.

Working from the top of your head gently taps with your knuckles all the way down to your neck, 'tapping in lines'.

After this, work your forehead with your finger tips push up and down working your fingers across your forehead also gently rotating your fingers on your temples.

Working down your body tapping, and rubbing. Then on down to your legs, and to your ankles. .

This will make you more receptive to the practice of the Tai Chi form///"Kata".

Within Reflexology, while we are down on the ankles it would be of interest to know some of the massaging pressure points on the feet. This is a great way of helping to relieve the tension and pain throughout the body.

For headaches, press your thumb and finger just below the big toenail. For the tension in the shoulders pinch and press, gently hold the point between the base of the fourth and fifth toes for about a count of five or six seconds. For sinus troubles squeeze the sides and back of each of your toes.

As you, get your-self fit; your mind begins to fall in place as well as a boost to your confidence.

Regular sessions of fitness that strengthens your heart and lungs can be very good for asthma sufferers; just a simple thing of getting fit can reduce your reliance on inhalers and can cut down on attacks.

Running, Cycling, Swimming, Martial arts & Tai-Chi, all these are good for you,

Chi-Kung breathing can also help.

The non-stop sequence of Chi-Kung breathing is giving the heart and lungs excellent exercise, correct breathing increases your lung capacity, and slows your heartbeat. It will make your cardiovascular system work much more efficiently.

Confidence grows and improves as you learn more, and draws on an inner strength to let you cope with most things in life.

This picture I took from the bottom of my garden, this is certainly universal energy.

Snake Creeps down.

Chi Kung Breathing.

One of the ways I get a class to feel the correct way of breathing through the stomach, (Tan-Tien) is to get them to lie on the floor, 'hands by their sides', just relax breathing naturally.

This will show you that the stomach muscles are the only ones that move in and out when you breathe. Pain or ailments, concentrated breathing will help you find your potent painful point. Close your eyes so you can focus the attention of your mind to the painful area. Try to Breathe deeply, imaging that you are breathing into the affected area.

'Pain or ailments':
Holding the point of pain with your hands, Very, gently rub them around the area, just like a mother with a child. When a child come running in from playing and hurt themselves, a mother will rub the spot and kiss it better. You are doing the self same thing with you own bodies healing process. So inhale deeply into the abdomen letting only your belly expands, 'not your chest'. Try to feel your breath deep down of your belly, and exhale slowly.

The energy you have pulled in will now circulate throughout the entire body. Focus your mind and breathe into the pained area for at least five to ten minutes.

Sensei Griffiths meditating On a Mountain in Wale's.

Tony Pandy, Penny Greaig

'Qigong sequences of which they're our many'.
To develop your internal strength and energy there are many Tan Tien breathing exercises.
One of the major ones we practice with in our group is in the standing horse stance, this stance for building leg muscles as well as finding your chi energy.
For those that are not up to such strenuous exercise, then the natural stance, will suffice, 'which is not so strenuous',

There are single arm waving as well as double arm waving. This will help you develop your internal strength and educate your body to find the correct way of moving in your Tai Chi.

To find your whole body motion, begin with the Tan Tien an inch below the navel with your concentrated breathing, the body is up right, try not to lean, bring you arms slowly up from your sides, to the front of your shoulders, extending your palms facing down & fingers pointing to the floor, as they come up, breathing in.
 When they reach shoulder level, bend wrists then push palms pushing as though your pushing along a table out away from the front of you, just as if you where pushing someone away from you, breathing out.

On breathing, as you breathe in the hands are moving in an upward motion, or coming towards you. As you breathe out your hands are either going away from you, or moving in a downward motion.

Whether one hand is going in opposite directions to the other, they are still equally balanced. Concentrating your energy and pushing out through the palms of your hands as you breathe out, exactly as you do in your Tai Chi.

A side kick. In the Chinese gardens, in Darling harbour Australia.

Universal energy: showing over my home.

The Rea Bridge House, a winter Sunset December, 2008.

One of my Tai Chi classes in Gloucestershire, England. One of my outstanding students on the left of the picture who is still practicing, Alex Bowen.

Chapter (24)

THE TAO

Tao, is the Chinese character approximately translated means, the way, as in the Do in Karate. It's the expression of a subtle concept which 'Lao Tzu'. The Taoist Sage of the sixth century B.C. said could not be spoken of, only lived.

Tao being the gentle pervasive power that follows the way. Means going along a path through nature's eternal changes. To acknowledge all living things that is the true essence of spirit. This is the harmony of man and woman that has the serenity inner peace. With all these things, this must be a healthy and corrective flourishing concept of all things good.

Interpreting the Tao is almost impossible. But it indicates a path to which we can travel from birth to death. But the path allows us to acknowledge to whom we are, and allows us to appreciate all living creatures to live in harmony, with them.

The Chinese arts are a form of health care, and healing to harmonies the human with Tao.   The Tao and your own chi energy with a mindful and trusting nature allowing your Chi to flow unimpeded leading to health in the body and spirit, to adjust readily to changing environmental and social circumstances.

Diseases or body ailments are the natural laws when falling out with the Tao. Losing the way means losing the ability of the body and mind and spirit, to adjust readily to changing environmental and circumstances.

Failures to adjust can cause constrictions and blockages, to and within your chi energy. Intervention, which increases vulnerability and disrupts the flow of vital and healing energy with this disruption the body, becomes diseased.

The mind becomes uneasy and the spirit withdraws and if the spirit completely withdraws, death will prevail.

The living of all individuals is unique and all aspects of Chinese medicines have to be complimented to that individual and treated accordantly.

White Lotus;
For loosening the neck muscles,

And shoulders muscles:

Hug a tree:

Wuji, Taiji, mabu,

Arms out stretched, in front, and in an ark, with arms shoulder width apart, palms facing inwards to the centre of mass, 'hugging a tree'.
Lower your knees keeping back upright (lower your centre mass).

Concentrate on your Tan tien, an inch below the nave. Close your eyes breathe (moving the stomach rather than the chest. (5 to 10 minutes).

Golden Lotus Dancing:

Lower hands to knees, (do not bend keep back strait) Reach down with feet flat then reach up going on tip toes pushing hands to the sky. Extending, your fingers open, then extending palms upwards. Then come back down and repeat, till you're comfortable with the amount you have given.
Rub hands together and wash face:
Rub hands together then rub face from bottom to top, outside to inside, rub nose gently with palm of hand in a circle.

Head tapping and shoulder rub:

Place one hand on the forehead; tap all over with the other hand in the hook position, wrist bent, all fingers and thumbs together in a point.

Put palms of hands over ears, with thumbs each side of neck Massage up and down the sides of the neck. Massage Trapezius (shoulders) squeeze, rub and tap on shoulders repeat sequence both sides.

Chapter (25)

Facts for fitness; Stamina, Suppleness, and Strength.

Stamina;
Are well-developed circulation, heart and muscle getting the right amount of oxygen where it is needed?
Suppleness;
Your neck; for your spine; joints, ligaments, and tendons, keeping you mobile. Important to stretch, and limber up before exercise.
Strength;
For strong muscles to strengthen your back for lifting, shoulders, trunk, thighs, and tummy.

Sensei Gerald Griffiths left, out running with some of his Students, 1982.

However, the best test for fitness is, 'stamina', keeping your rhythmic large group of muscle moving for a sustained period and often, building up your fitness gradually week by week. 'Maybe even walking first, train with a friend, or with a well run club

Holding an ordinary conversation while running, shows that you're breathing is quit regulated and that you are not breathless. Building up to more jogging, than walking.
The best time of day is when you feel good to do so. (Not after a heavy meal). Exercise can be bad for you, during or just after a cold-flu, or when you are tired, or painful joints. When you have a fever or aches and pain, this could only make matters worse.

In the summer time the sunshine helps. The brighter days get you in the mood and you're more likely to feel more full of energy and ready to exercise. When hot you won't feel as hungry or in the need for comfort food. Studies show cortical drops during summer, (cortical are linked to the storage of abdominal fats).

It's known the brain's serotonin drops during winter, hence the winter blues. And of course in the summer you have lighter evenings to do more outside activities. Cycling is very good; cycling can burn 300 calories per half hour, at 10 miles an hour, good for toning bottom and legs.
Getting out in the garden, pulling up weeds, and mowing the grass. You'l burn about 140 calories an hour weeding, and a 220 mowing. (Watch your back).

A question that was once asked of me was how you get to stop a stitch, when you are running, without stopping, or interrupting your run. Just slow down, take your time in warming up. Try more stretching exercises before you start your run. The stitch is a way of telling you, you are not getting enough blood flow to your internal organs. The blood flow has been diverted to the larger muscle group you started to use, when you started your run.

Obviously as your fitness improves, you will find the severity of the stitch will be reduced. This is why you must start slowly. As your fitness increases, the actual level of blood flow will have more time to change. A good rise in temperatures is sufficient to allow your muscle tissue to allow more flow, making your muscles that much more flexible for your training session.

Running is one of the most popular forms of exercise, running is every good for your lungs, they work that much harder, generating about ten time that much more lung capacity, using the oxygen into your blood stream and with regular jogging will increases your cardious-cular system.

Nevertheless, running does have down falls. Running can be the most high impact, as the feet hits the ground, the impact on your body is about five or six times your body weight, it reverberates up your legs and spine. 'Not so good on your knees and spinal joints'.

Sensei Griffiths on the Running machine age 65.

Staying focused can be challenging in its self, and to keep a positive outlook and sense of achievement and self-worth and self-esteem, it is very important to keeping yourself fit.

The fact is; if you are in old age there is still no excuse for laziness, shunning exercise will make you more vulnerable to being more over weight, which is then a vicious circle, the more over weight you become the more lazy you fill and so on, so you need to start giving it a go, however old you are, it's never too late.

I myself am now 68 at the start of writing this book and hope to go on exercising for the rest of my life.

The best types of exercises' are the one that will help your heart. Which are more aerobic activities and any repetitive, rhythmic exercise that involves the larger muscle groups, the legs, shoulders and arms; here are some examples, walking, cycling, swimming and dancing, the activity of aerobics will increase the bodies intake of oxygen, which adds the work load of your heart and lungs, making the blood and heart circulation more efficient, helping your stamina.

It is always very special to warm up gradually every session, and if you are just starting out, building up slowly, in addition, after an illness or layoff. With these down falls it is very important to wear the correct footwear running shoes is quite different from the shoes in the gym.

Running shoes is more adequate, cushioning, and durability; Inadequate footwear can be blamed for most trouble to cartilage damage knee joints, and a good pair will protect your feet from blisters.

As warming up is important, so is warming down. The sweating of our body's are ways of cooling down the body's natural protection of overheating. When we over heat a message is sent from our brains to a nerve, which passes signals to our sweet glands, which is the tinny glands in the skins surface. These glands in the skin then leak water which evaporates to cool you down. So by cooling down with your exercises is just as important, and drink plenty of water when training.

**Arrowed: Sensei Griffiths done the Gloucester Marathon,
in four hours forty minutes 4th October 1981**

Chapter (26)
CRAMP AND MUSCLE SPASM WHEN TRAINING

On just starting out, 'if in doubt', before all vigorous exercise you should consult a doctor, especially in your later years.

Lunges are and can be good prior to and leading up to running; adapt a good posture standing up straight, take a long step forward, bending your front knee over your toes. Keep back straight as good as you can, back heel of the floor. Step back and repeat the other side. Good to do during and after or prior to a brisk walk or running; repeat two or three times.

Cramps occur when a muscle contracts and wont stretch back out again. This often happens during training and exercising.

So it's very important during training to stop whatever you are doing immediately. Try massaging the muscle to stretch out again, you should be able to find where the cramp is as the muscle will feel very hard and very lumpy, even some twitching. Cramp will often occur if you have not warmed up and done your stretching exercises properly.

Some ache and cramps could be due to the fact you may have been doing exercise and using muscle that you have not recently development using muscle you have not used before, if you have been going to the Gym or exercising or standing for long periods, this can sometimes cause cramps.

It probably means that muscles you have not used before are being strained and the aching is due to stiffness. You need to get your legs moving as soon as you can. When the muscle is used they produce lactic acids in your legs which, if it isn't't absorbed by the body, they will ache. To get rid of these acids you will have to get the muscles going again. So start with some stretches to loosen them up.

If cramp happens frequently there may be deficiencies in your diet of Potassium and calcium. By combating this, eat plenty of Bananas and Pineapple; Drink plenty of milk and fluids.

I was reading something somewhere also that some foods are naturally anti-inflammatory; they can help in relieving pain and serious illnesses in long term inflammation turns to pain.

So pack your diet with nuts, seeds, oily fish, pulses, berries and broccoli. Vitamins from these are (A, C, E, B1, and 12) the Minerals (selenium, zinc and Magnesium) Omega fat eases pain and inflammation. Nuts and pulses raise the level of feel good endorphins that cope with pain. Blueberries contain proanthocyanidins, which are anti-inflammatory expelling toxic body fluids that make inflammation painful.

Pain does not always equal harm, but pain is a message, telling you there is something wrong. The pain messages in simplest form, the theory are as follows: nerves from all parts of your body runs to the spinal cord, which is the main meeting point for your nervous system.

The spinal cord has a series of gateways of gates that exists through which pain messages pass from all over the body which passes through to the brain these gate can be opened or closed to varying degrees and amounts of pain to be experienced, and how bad the injury is.

Some pain can even make you fill nausea and faintness. Some pains can be brought on by stress and tension and thinking about your pain can make it worse, you need to be relaxed and try to distract yourself from it by doing something interesting and enjoyable. The aim being is to give more control over the pain problem. Rest by all means, but keeping still and avoiding no movement, can be more harmful.

The first few days after an injury by having pain makes you rest, this allows you the healing process to start. Common causes of acute pain are usually, a sprained, or a strain on a ligament or tissues, which is connected to your bones and joints, a strain is usually of are muscles and tendons

With any physical activity, injuries still happen, so it is important to know how you will deal with them. Sports and exercise injuries fall into a couple of categories. There are very acute injuries, which can happen like sprained ankles, or a torn muscle. 'Chronic injuries'. Which are the result of unaccustomed exercise or can be from excessive exercise? Many acute injuries to joints, muscles, tendons and ligaments cause bleeding, swelling and pain. Healing with these injuries, you should stop exercising immediately.

For example a sprained ankle, you would find it very difficult to walk for a few days because of the pain. You would have to rest to start the healing to begin.

A sprained ankle is caused when ligaments holding together the ankle bone tear or stretch. Which some times are hard and longer healing than some bone brakes, Ice packs straight away and rest is the answer.

You need to apply Ice; one method is;
Step one; prepare two tubs of water one ice cold the other one tipped or bearably hot;
Step two; sitting on a chair place your foot in cold tub to reduce swelling for two minutes;
Step three; place hot alternates between tubs five six times finally with the cold one.
Step four; dry foot rubbing softly with towel. Then rest.

Precautions on using an ice pack
Never put an ice pack directly to the skin always use a damp towel or cloth this will prevent ice burns. Only use an ice pack on areas of your skin where there are no open wounds or grazes, and the skin feels normal, where you can feel hot or cold sensations. And not where the area has poor blood circulation. Do not leave ice pack on too long, no longer than two minutes.

Gerald Running in the Gloucester Marathon, 1981.

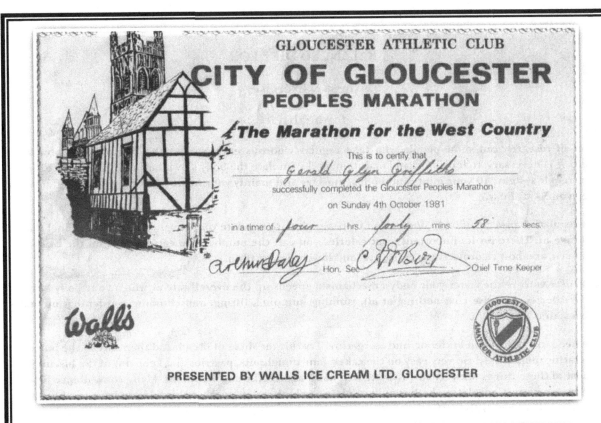

GLOUCESTER ATHLETIC CLUB

CITY OF GLOUCESTER
PEOPLES MARATHON

The Marathon for the West Country

This is to certify that

Gerald Glyn Griffiths

successfully completed the Gloucester Peoples Marathon

on Sunday 4th October 1981

in a time of *four* hrs. *forty* mins. *58* secs.

Arthur Daley Hon. Sec. *C W Birt* Chief Time Keeper

Walls

PRESENTED BY WALLS ICE CREAM LTD. GLOUCESTER

Sensei Griffiths running in the Gloucester Marathon, 4th October 1981.

Chapter (27)

A BALANCED DIET FOR

Fitness & exercise,

for health.

A lot of research can show people who take regular vigorous exercise, cut the risk of heart attacks. Exercise is necessary, to look after and maintain, and stimulate the body's own natural maintenance, and your repair system. All your joints and bones, muscles and mainly your heart will keep you young, if you keep your body busy.

The regulation process of input and output is to stay slim, to regulate your weight, to burn more fuel than you take in. There for its important what calories you eat, the number you eat depends on the calories you burn, and how rigorous the exercise are, and how long you train.

The fitter you are the faster your body's mechanism speeds up the overall rate at which your body burns these calories. Exercise cost nothing at all, running, jumping, lifting, and climbing, gardening, up and down stairs.

The need to cut down on butter or, and margarine. Try thicker slices of bread, and then spread the butter-margarine more thinly. Go very easy on the cakes, jam' doughnuts, pastries and keep out of the biscuit jar – most of these things are very surprisingly rich in fat as well the sugar content. Many convenience foods go the same way. Chocolate: whether milk or plain are high in fat; nearly a third. If you have to, there are now slimming types with low fat.

Eating less red meat: A meal can be just as exciting and nourishing without meat. In fact, you can get all the protein and other nutrients you need without eating meat at all. Personally, I do like meat, so I do try to keep to most white meats, as they normally have less fat.

If you do eat meat then choose a nice leaner cut, always cut of the fatty bits, and maybe change to chicken. It is far less fatty than most other meats, and a lot cheaper. Sheppard's pie, with lots of vegetables; Use boiled or baked potatoes, rice, beans.

Try to keep away from fry-ups. Fry-up's can have large quantities of fat; try to grill instead of frying, letting all the grease drain away.

Pasta's are very good using vegetable oil, spaghetti Bolognese. Eating fish instead of meat. White fish preferably, it has less fat. 'Definitely not covered in batter'.

Definitely no to cream. Double dairy cream is nearly half – fat. Most yogurts instead, and skimmed milk rather than full milk. Low fat cheeses, slimmer type and soft cheese is much better for you.

All suggestions, I hope I have been able to help you with, remember concentrated fat in your blood stream, will knock up your cholesterol, due to bad eating habits. Your body-machine must get the right nutrients, and nourishment, and each person's body-chemistry (metabolism) is different.

Eating a very varied diet is important, so you do not go short of proteins vitamins, fibro, and minerals that your body needs.

The amount of energy foods in your every day diet, do not necessarily mean you will get more energetic. Personally, if I train hard I find I can eat most things I enjoy. Nevertheless, it is still important to have variety in your diet. Plenty of fresh fruit vegetables, and cereals, fish, eggs meat, and dairy products, which will contain all the vitamins you need.

Recently in a journal annual of oncology, some Italian scientists said an apple every day claims to keep breast ovary and prostate tumours away, making you up to 20 percent less likely to develop these cancers. More than one apple reduces your chances of cancer of the mouth, gullet, bowel, or throat by up to 40 per cent.

Researches by Oklahoma State University in the US say dried plums may stave off osteoporosis. And munching them regularly stops bones thinning, probably due to the antioxidants in the fruit. A study in life science magazine it is said that, Rhubarb is also a very good thing, this helps improve circulation, stops blood sticking to the artery walls and is very good as an anti-inflammatory.

Bananas are known to ward of exhaustion, and have loads of vitamins, so these are very good for you to.

Modern-day science has proved folklore has held true. For 5000 years Garlic medicinal use, has been used for bites, tumours, wounds, headaches and heart disease, today the list is longer.

Being defined as an herb belonging to the onion family its clove's contains two sets of nutrients, water, soluble nutrients, includes vitamins, enzymes, amino, acids and natural sugars. It is the sulphur containing amino acids that have antioxidants properties. This proves with modern day science that folklore has held true.

It also helps fight against Arteriosclerosis and lower cholesterol, and has a mild effect on hypertension. It thins the blood and is pretty good to keeping your arteries open and cardiovascular system, significantly lowering mildly elevated blood pressure, improving blood flow by making blood more fluid, blood cells less sticky, and platelets less agreeable. .... Influencing the blood-clotting system so dissolve if there is a cause obstruction. It prevents irregular heartbeats and injury of cells when there is a shortage of oxygen. Thus limiting the ability of cells in the vessel walls to grow, multiply and form arteriosicertotic lesions.

"Nutrition's", "dehydration", and "performance".

To help with your Chi energy to flow unhindered a healthy balanced diet is essential for good health. This is whether you're an elite habitual athlete, or just enjoy exercise; we need to avoid fatigue and dehydration.

Whatever your sport or exercise regime by making informed dietary choices you can optimize your training to improve your performance.

To help fit or control your weight the principles are the same. The key is healthy balanced diet in moderation, maybe extra carbohydrates, if you are a regular exercise.

When you are training and your training program is more physically demanding you must consider the nutrients that will assist in your recovery between training sessions.

The nutrition's can influence performance at all levels. Taking the advice from all resources. Turning the theory in to practice is challenging, making time to eat, plan, and prepare. No matter the types of exercise you do the body uses some glucose for energy. The main sources of glucose being carbohydrates sugars and starches.

We all know to drink plenty of fluids every day to stay fully hydrated. The body muscles use a lot of water. Twenty five percent of energy, the rest is released as heat, making your body hot causing evaporation, sweating releasing the bodies' fluids so it's so important to top up during training.

In general we need to drink about two litres of fluid a day to be hydrated. Watching the colour of the urine is a good indicator of fluid loses, if pale and plentiful you are well hydrated. If the colour is dark and sparse you will need more fluids and will affect your performance to do well, and all these things can hinder the flow of your Chi energy.

A BALANCED DIET TO LOSE WEIGHT AND STAY FIT AND Healthy

EATING HABITS. Your Eating habits can be spoiling your diet and weight, eating is not just what you eat, but why, how, where and when. This is the key factor when trying to slim.

When you are bored or even stressed you eat to try to distract yourself from these feelings. Sugar treats like chocolate and sweet things get you sort of happy.

If you wish to change these feelings you need to look at the Emotional side and not your stomach. Be very careful on going out for a coffee with a friend – For if you decide to have a Milky blended coffee you will be adding an extra 700 calories to that days intake, stick to tea or coffee with just a little milk. Crisps food snacks has high Salt contents, which is tempting when out for coffee; go more for a small muesli bar which would be more healthy.

Music and walking or cycling will help distract you from your stomach and stimulate the brain and give you a buzz, but with no calories.

Some green leafy vegetables contain chemicals called Phosphatidylserine, such as spinach and green cabbage, which is very good for maintaining a healthy brain this will help the metal functions and memory, which could reduce levels of the stress hormones cortical. Oily fish also contains D.H.A. an essential fatty acid which is a very vital part to building blocks for a healthy brain. Taking some supplements to help maintain brain functions and performance such as Vitadiotics menopace, Neurozan, this provides concentrated D.H.A. together to complete a spectrum of nutrients.

The emotional feelings you would get from eating food only last a few minutes, but by the things I have suggested, will last much longer and much more rewarding and worth it.

When sitting down you will probably eat less, the body will register calories much more when you are actually having a sit down meal, than on the run, or standing. Try to keep the biscuits tin out of sight, taking temptation away, take tempting things of the shelf's in your fridge and cupboards. Don't forget, drinks contain calories to, even flavoured drinks contain calories. Plain water is fine and will help fill you up. Starting by smaller portions and know how much is enough, try a smaller plate to put your food on.

Night time nibbling is the worst time, late night snacks before going to bed to sleep, not only can keep you awake, but will increases your calories intake.

Try not to eat watching Television; you can eat so much more calories this way. Only focus on your food at proper meal times and try to keep to it. You will be more likely to binge eat if you leave long hours between meals, your bodies are designed to eat every 3 to 4 hours, so don't skip meals and keep to a regular routine. If you have to eat between meals try low fat yogurts or fruit or a small handful of nuts.

A Balanced Diet to be able to lose weight and stay fit and healthy.

Your diet not only effects your weight but what you eat is an impact on your emotions in all areas of your health, food can reduce your (cholesterol) levels by about 5 to 10 percent.

For a few years after the Menopause you have four or five times more chances to contract heart disease, the estrogens protects and helps your heart which helps balance the levels of good, and bad cholesterols in your blood the estrogens can drop as you reach the menopause so the risks of cholesterol and heart disease goes up. Keeping bad cholesterol low and keeping good cholesterol high by a very good healthy diet.

Cholesterol heart related disease causes around 117,000 deaths every year and about more than 2, 5 million. UK people live with these diseases Cholesterol is caused by all the types of fats I have already explained here. But some types of fats are essential for good health (sounds like a contradiction), but if levels get so high it builds up in the artery walls thus increasing the risk of heart problems and even strokes. It is usually caused by a diet of high saturated fats a lack of exercise or drinking too much alcohol. If you have a hereditary of heart attacks, you're probably at a higher risk if there is someone in your immediate family who is a sufferer. It is much more Prevalent in the over 45's, but it is becoming more common amongst the younger people and their life styles.

When I was young and growing up we had no televisions or computers and tendo games. We played outside. So we were much fitter as children, than the kids today. Today's life style of kids today is far less healthy. Recent Studies show, thousands of children in America and the UK were obese with clogged arteries and high levels of Cholesterol. Cholesterol doesn't show any symptoms, so if you think you're at risk have a blood test and do something about it. The Cholesterol that is carried through your body in the blood as lipoproteins, by eating and by cutting back on saturated fats, biscuits, red meat, cheese and butter, try to enjoy more monounsaturated fats which you get in olive oil avocados and oily fish, many breakfast cereals are high in sugar and salt. Go more for Porridge, muesli, or eggs on toast and delicious nutritious treats like nuts and fruit.

If you like toast for breakfast you may wish to change to Rye bread. University Scientist found that people that eat Rye bread in the mornings were less hungry before and after their Lunch than people that had ate a typical wheat bread breakfast. Benefits come from Rye's high fiber content, 'nice with scrambled Eggs'. We know it is hard to break lifelong habits.

When you are very young, sometimes, most times, you are running around here there and everywhere, so your calories are being burnt up at a greater rate. As you grow and get older, you won't be running around as much as you use to. So stop talking about losing weight and actually do it, but do it sensibly. We are always going on about going on a Diet tomorrow, never getting around to it. If you want to get slimmer you will need to find out what you should be eating for the life you are leading, as in Fitness, how many times you go to the Gym or go Running; and then get started, maybe get a healthy eating plan that suits your life style.

But don't just go cold turkey, slowly cut out your fatty foods and onto fruit and vegetables and start slowly, one meal at a time. Try not to skip Breakfast. Poached eggs on whole meal or wholegrain cereal, fat free natural yogurts.

By eating plenty of fruit and vegetables low fat dairy and lots of wholegrain cutting down on salt and red and processed meats could reduce your risk of kidney stones by 40 to 50 per cent which is linked to Hypertension and diabetes.

Doing an exercise class or going for a power walk with friends rather than walking alone. Will produce more feel good endorphin which will dull pain as well as help you lose weight and get fit? An apple a day or just before each meal will help you eat less. Sucking mints can hold back hunger pangs between your meals. Lots of certain fruit and vegetables are low in energy but eating lots of pasta, potatoes, rice, eggs and fish, you can still loss weight as they are very high content of water.

Your kidneys are there to filter your blood that removes waste products and excess fluid from your body. They are also there to produce hormones that can help maintain healthy blood pressure. So to keep them in top shape is so important.

On kidney failure you would need a kidney transplant and could face years of painful Dialysis while waiting for a donor. In your middle age, your kidneys can become less efficient and the risk of renal failure can rise as you get older.

Some of the early signs and symptoms to look out for is, feeling tired, difficulty with your concentration, itchy skin, being breathless, poor appetite, nausea, and your weight can drop, you should go to your doctor immediately for a test. You are most at risk if you have high blood pressure, Diabetes, vascular disease, and a family history of kidney disease. Your doctor GP will give you blood and urine test to check your kidney functions, 'once again', keeping a healthy sensible health plan. The role of our intestines is to selectively absorb the nutrients required by the body and to reject those materials that should not be absorbed, such as toxins and metabolic by products, with 80 tons of food passing through our intestines in a life time it is clear how important a big massive task they have.

Next to a balanced diet and regular physical activity you can actually support your intestines with your effective eating habits.

There is some evidence, garlic helps in the prevention of cancer particularly in to the stomach, colon, bladder, breast, and oesophageal variety.

40, 000 women were studied after a four year period included large amounts of garlic in their diet, they were less likely to have developed colon cancer by 30%, this could have been abtribulated to all life style diet, garlic was a common factor. We all need more energy we would love to be able to bounce out of bed in the mornings and keep going all day. But it is so hard to fill good like it all the time.

As our levels of energy declines as we grow older, harder to sleep, hard to get up, end in a vicious circle which is hard to break ending up getting lazy. Then losing muscle mass. So a very healthy life style is so important, it is inevitable you get older and tired.

Craving Chocolate, but trying to be healthy, grabbing a slice of cake or having seconds, which is just emotion. Chewing food more slowly and properly helps improve the work of your digestive enzymes. This helps to break down and digest your meals more easily. Brown rice, sweet potato, broccoli and apples, pineapple, yogurt and soups. Help to make you feel fuller for longer.

Avoid sugar, sweeteners, fizzy drinks, alcohol and caffeine.

The worst fats are Trans fats, fatty Trans acids are so bad for you, why are they put in the manufactures products and food. (What are they?) Tran's fats are made when hydrogen is added to vegetable oil a process called Hydrogenation or partial Hydrogenation. The fat then stays solid at higher temperatures and then lengthens the shelf life of food products. But the thing is it can shorten your own shelf life, by eating them.

The F.D.A. requires all manufactures must list the amount of Tran's fats that are used. There is controversy over whether Tran's fatty acids are even worse than artery-clogging saturated fats. Experts believe, according to other health authorities they are as, or just as bad as saturated fats, but no worse.

Scientist at a University in America recently reported that Diets rich in Tran's fats may cause a redistribution of fat tissue into the abdomen, (which is the worst place to store fat for both your health and appearance), leading to a greater higher body weight, even if the total calories are the same.

So for the bottom line to the degree you must reduce your intake of saturated fat and Trans fatty acids to reduce your risk of heart attacks and many other illnesses. The dietary guidelines of Americas heart association recommends cutting saturated fat no less than seven percent of calories and Tran's fat to no less than one percent of total calories in your diet.

But realistically most people will not calculate the Saturated-Fat, Tran's-Fats in their diets each day.

So trying to protect yourself, you need to eat less Red meat and dairy products, as well as tropical oils, coconut oils, palm oil, commercially prepared cookies, cakes, crackers and most snack foods. If the label says Hydrogenated, avoid it; steer clear of foods that contain more than three grams of Tran's fats or saturated fats on a serve.

Chapter 28

The health risks of smoking

In addition, to

The fitness you wish to obtain

Sensei, Gerald Griffiths.

Smoking as a young man of 24 years.

I use to smoke as you can see, and during my time in the armed forces, although I was very fit, I can remember being in a cross country run, against some of the forces top athletes.

I was leading the field on a high, way out in front on the last three or four hundred yards my competitors were catching me up, I had to increase the pace, which was very hard on my lungs, I was really gasping for air, as we approached the finish line, there was not a lot in it, but I did not have the breath needed to go up a pace, and on looking back, had I not smoked I would have won instead of coming second. This happened so much in many of my Army training and fitness levels.

Soldiers when training would be told OK, "smoke brake".

My turning point was after I came out of the forces I was driving for a living, as in Trucks and Articulated trucks. Of course sitting down all day in a truck did not help. I remember finishing work and on the Bell I used to run up a load of steps to the car park to be out first. I use to get halve way and had to stop to catch my breath, this was when I made up my mind to stop.

So as you can see from my pictures here, I was a smoker, but when I was twenty nine to thirty years old I managed to give them up. This was not easy I was on about forty to fifty a day, being abroad in the armed forces the cigs were cheap as they were duty free.

But I managed it because I was so determined to give them up, I used to be looking in my pockets for but ends and it took me about a year, to nearly two years to finely give them up, so glad I did, for after a few years my lungs were much better in my breathing, my Martial art and fitness improved no end.

So from this I would like to help you pack up,

so read carefully think and take this in.

As a Martial arts instructor, it is my responsibility to discourage and point out the dangers of smoking.

Smoking contains numerous additives and harmful substances at least two of which contributes to heart disease. The nicotine makes the heart beat faster, and pushes up the blood pressure.

Carbon monoxide, which is a poisonous gas, cut down the amount of oxygen the blood, can carry. The health risks in smoking do decrease dramatically on giving up.

Smoking, stress, obesity and too much salt can make matters worse. Doctors will measure your blood pressure at its highest and lowest points as your heartbeats and then relaxes. Anyone with blood pressure above 140 over 90 is classed as having high blood pressure (hypertension). Remember that ignoring the warning signs on a fag packet is such a danger to your health; they are not put there for just any old reason.

The government recognizes the need for this, the evidence linking smoking and lung cancer is overwhelming. Even one puff on a cigarette can weaken the lungs and the ability to defend them-selves from infections. The lungs are made-up of spongy tissues that has to be-able to stretch, contract and constrict, as you breathe. Relieving the blood of carbon dioxide and waste.

Returning fresh oxygen to this spongy tissue impregnating and enritchin'ing the blood stream.

The bronchial tubes will carry this air deep into your lungs by smaller and smaller tubes until the air reaches the alveoli.

The millions of alveoli tissues in each lung exchange the oxygen and the carbon dioxide. The haemoglobin, (The tissue molecules that is binding holding the oxygen in the air sacs), where the carbon dioxide is then exhaled.

These tiny tissues can be all clogged up with tar and nicotine, and the inhaled cigarette smoke is an irritating gas and particles causing anything that will slow down this intricate process will damage your heath dramatically

The risks of smoking do decrease dramatically on giving up. You can have many reasons for giving up; the terrible smell, the high risks to health, the high cost involved, and the lack of fitness, and the effect on every day illnesses of serious diseases.

Pneumonia is of inflammation of the tissues in your lungs. It can affect one or both side of your chest. It can be caused by a virus, a bacteria parasite or a Fungus;

People can get pneumonia following cold or other chest infections, and around one in ten people die from it in each year, it's much more common in women of over 60 to 70 year olds.

I keep going back to fitness, keeping yourself fit is the first line of defending against it, again as I keep repeating your diet must be full of immune-boosting vitamins and mineral, that will help fight any viruses that you may catch.

Be determined to keep flu at bay for the winter, you will need to be washing your hands on a regular basis, Germs on your hands are one of the worst ways to catch colds and flu, just a couple of minutes to wash your hands use hot water with plenty of soap washing thoroughly between your fingers and under nails and your wrist. Bugs thrive in moist places and in the warm.

If you take regular exercise,

If you smoke, you need to quit.   **SAY NO MORE you have been warned**

See the clock at the top of picture, you're life is ticking away, don't shorten it.

It is known that 30.000 people die every year from (C.O.P.D.) Chronic Obstructive airways caused by smoking. Coughing up the phlegm is an important sign of C.O.P.D; and the breathless-ness just on a mild activity, which does not help in trying to ward of coughs and colds of winter.

Smoking damages your lungs and makes them much more likely to get infected, you must take Pneumonia seriously, STOP SMOKING, if you become unwell with fever, chest pains, and coughing bouts, you need to see your doctor strait away. And in the UK if your over sixty five you are entitled to pneumonia jab with your regular Flu jab, which you need to take advantage of to reduce your risks.

You can have many reasons for giving up; the terrible smell, the high risks to health, the high cost involved, and the lack of fitness, and the effect on every day illnesses of serious diseases.

Studies show Ex-smokers and non-smokers feel less anxious depression and stressed than a long term smoker. In the long term of smoking, nicotine dulls the brain pleasure receptors. Occasional smoking doubles your risk of lung cancer and heart attacks even four or five cigarettes a day raise your risk, of smoking related diseases.

None smokers living with smokers have a 23% raised risk of heart disease and Lung cancer. While it is also a cause of cot deaths, asthma and ear infections in children.

If you are smoking around children, there is a good chance they could contract Asthma which is a condition that affects the airways. Small tubes which carry air to the airways, in and out of the lungs, if your child has asthma at a very young age, it could, or will continue throughout his, her, life, there airways will become sensitive and inflamed. If a child comes in contact with something that irritates there airways, this will trigger an asthma attack, which will narrow the airways making it difficult to breath. Then the muscle around the walls of the airways will start to tighten and become inflamed, mucus that cleans and protects the lining of the airways will build up and can get in the way of air trying to reach their lungs.

Children will more than likely develop Coughs and wheezes, particularly at night or after exercises, or when they have a cold. The wheezing and coughing and being breathless are more first thing in the mornings. Reliever inhalers will help to relieve most of these symptoms.

And will have to be kept with them at all-time. You will need to work in partnership with their school. Making sure there school knows your child has Asthma.

If you are teaching Martial arts and fitness, especially to young children, your induction papers will need to have all these questions to answer on the induction forms. 'This is your responsibility'. Also to make sure you know what to do in an emergency if that child needs help. You have a legal duty to carry out risk assessments within your club. You must keep very accurate records to comply with the government's health & Safety regulations.

Self Employed instructors have the same responsibility and rights as an Employer. Your insurance cover needs to be completely up to date but you need to comply with all the needs of the rule's and regulations' of safety, to have complete cover.

'There will be no excuses if you do not'. Your cover can become invalid.

Smoking can dehydrate the skin, breaks down the collagen, and stains teeth. Smoking impairs wound healing for your own natural body's repair.

In pregnant women every time they smoke a cigarette it increases your baby's heart beat faster, smoke passes though your lungs and into your bloodstream, which you share with your baby, it reduces the amount of oxygen your baby receives affecting its development.

Male smokers are twice as likely to become impotent than non-smokers. While female smokers take longer to conceive.

There are still over 13 million lighting up in the UK alone. Figures revel that 66% of smokers want and try to give up. Which is not surprising as there are over 115.000 smoking – related deaths per year in the UK and 30% of all cancers that

Are linked to smoking. Premature aging and other bad health illnesses are all conducive to smoking.

Smoking tips to help to give up:

As many as six or seven smoker wish to give up and be smoke free: (HOW).

Start by telling all your friends and family you're going to do so. Try to pick a day;

You must have motivational support within your home life, because you cannot rely on will power alone. There are lots of help aid today, not like when I packed up, (if I can do it you can). There are patches and gum, micro tabs inhalators, and more to help with nicotine addiction.

You may have a local Medicare or local help team where staff with expert professionals who will be only to please to help you go smoke free. There advisers will be able to give you individual level of addiction and advice you on the best treatments to help you quit.

When you are having a hard time and think about giving up think of the reasons you wanted to give up in the first place. you will go through these withdraw symptoms so you will need some incentive, think of the ailments and illnesses cigarettes can give, that I have pointed out to you. If you have children think of them, and of your own health and how it will affect your well being, and how it will affect you.

GOOD LUCK YOU CAN DO IT.

I have been on television with my art Alison Holloway a television News reader came to my home and I was on the Box for about thirty minutes, on H.T.V. west, Most of the session was on the Long staff of which I fill very competent in.

Chapter (29)

This is an interview; for international worldwide magazine,

Sensei Gerald Griffiths 6th Dan giving opinions of the martial arts

Which aspects of martial arts practice do you enjoy most?

Over all, practice is what I enjoy most.

Do you enjoy kata (forms, competition) free sparing/ did you always enjoy them and if not did you come to enjoy them?

Yes to them all, over all practice is what I enjoy most. However, Sampon kumeti was a good turning point in my practice. The way we practice with sampon was obviously to improve technique. We strove for harmony with a partner with distance, timing and breathing with a strong mental intent. However, I do enjoy all my practices; "kata, kumeti" and warm-ups.

What is it especially about them that you like?

Kata and the importance from one complicated move to another

What successes/ promotions have you achieved?

Well I did competitions for a short while. I came 3rd in the Tera-Karate-kai International championships for over forties' and came 2nd the following year. I am now a Shihan and a Master in Tai-Chi and The chief instructor for our group.

How important is achieving? Which is more important: the satisfaction at having achieved something or the admiration of others? (Please be truthful)

I get self-satisfaction if I achieve a good technique, or if I perform a good kick, ECT; However, being very truthful, I do get satisfaction if someone said they enjoyed watching me perform this kata, or that kata, ECT; if people admire you then, "as an instructor", they will listen to what you have to say with your teaching, and will want to practice with you. I do enjoy singing and have sung with a band, "I am a karaoke presenter", and if a person says they enjoyed this song, or that song, or my singing, it is the same admiration as my karate. "I must admit I do get a buzz by both.

How important is realism to martial practice?

Realism', it could never be completely real until you have to use it in the street. In the Do-Jo, you are looking for a good technique. Some practices are not practical for street defence as practiced on their own, but put them all together over all, will then become practical on the street, " Even warm-ups for your fitness, ECT:

If you imagine your separate techniques and different practices as different colour's put them all in a pot, stir them up create one colour then you have realism and self-defence. "It's all there.

How important is understanding, the purpose behind moves/techniques? How do you find out about those purposes? "From your teacher or from your own study? Which do you think is the best way to find out?

Of course it is important to understand what a move is for, to know what you are doing. A good teacher will explain what the moves are for, and must show it effectively, but then it is important to study for yourself, over and over, until it becomes your own and second nature. It is like showing someone how to ride a bike. You can sit on it like this way or that way, show how to turn the pedals ECT; nevertheless, the person learning to ride has to get on it and practice until he, or she, has mastered balance and confidence in riding it themselves.

It is a case of practice makes perfect and the best way to find out is to keep practicing, as your instructor shows you the way. (Karate-Do).

Has your training changed in content or emphasis since you started? If so then why has it changed?

When I first took up karate, it was for fighting ability. Now I train for the enjoyment it gives me. It improves my mind and body and it keeps me communicating with young people and having something to give back.

Youngsters at ten or twelve that trained with me, still train now that they are adults, but are also bringing their sons and daughters along to train as well. To teach and see these kids now grown up and responsible adults- 'well this gives me the greatest buzz'.

As in content, yes I do now practice quite a lot of Tai-Chi as this improves my Karate, on leaning the yin and yan (soft and hard of body posture.

What does it take to make a success of martial arts practice?

Dedication to practice, (time) and making time, "Obviously hard work".

List the physical /mental requirements that you need to succeed in your practice?

Doing my best to improve my physical ability, leg stretching to keep supple especially as you get older and a strong mind and concentration .

Which requirements do you think most people lack?

Outside of martial arts, or for beginners, I think people lack "discipline and fitness", Fitness is improving and people are eating more sensibly these days. However, many people out there are overweight.

I like my food but over the last couple of years I have been watching what I eat; Chinese food "yummy", prawns sea food, the way Chinese people cook them with lots of high cholesterol ingredient – all the nice things seem that way. Back to your question; discipline, fitness and dedication is what people lack.

What can you do to get round physical drawbacks such as small body mass and low flexibility?

Well I do not know how you can say that a small body mass is a drawback. If you look at most Japanese men and women they are quite small people. Look at Bruce Lee who is a good example.

One of my black belts Bob Huntley who is a 5th Dan. His body mass is small and there is not an ounce of fat on him. He would certainly not think it is a drawback, in fact he would think the opposite, - "built for speed" "however", and you do need flexibility.

Is a large body mass important in terms of martial effectiveness?

Depends if you mean large body mass of muscle or fat. Sure if you are large and muscular it can be effective but only if you are flexible and fluent and fit. That does not mean a big man will always overcome a small one.

It is possible for a big man in a grabbling situation. But then the American Grace Brothers in the ultimate fighting rings where quite small, and they domineered, the fight world for some time.

Do you measure effectiveness in martial practice through winning competitions? Or through gaining grades? Alternatively, through working the door?

Through working the door'. We as a group do not enter competitions so personally with us it can't be that, also I don't think it's gaining grades, although it does go to show what level of practice a student has achieved through out his/her practice and gives them incentive to achieve more. Most of all the other things like hard work, good technique and working the door. If a club instructor has a very large club, he must be doing something right. Techniques, must work' and be practical. If shown to work then people would want to join your club. "Good technique" and a good teacher

What is the most important spin-of of martial practice?

Group participation; friendships; fitness; respect for others. The character rounding aspects, of confidence, body management. Producing good kids, and keeping them off the streets.

How effective are martial arts in the street situation? How might they be made more effective? Do you cover all aspects of practice _ striking, grabbling, locks ECT? If not which are omitted and why?

Martial arts in the street. Well we are all vulnerable however good we become; but, yes martial arts are only as good as the person that practices it and it's only as good as you keep practicing .

In our practice, we will use any technique that shows to be practical and steal from any style or practice that will improve our own practice. We will omit nothing.

Which is more important – determination to succeed or physical skills as power and flexibility?

Determination to succeed; without that you will not find skill, or power and flexibility to succeed

Martial arts' training improves physical requirements such as flexibility and power. Can it also develop a mental requirements and if so, how?

Yes, it can. Your overall practice will develop mental requirements. There are many practices that do and to many to mention here. Mainly one practice on its own will not develop mental attitude, but put together will develop mental attitude, doing sampon kumite very slowly and practiced with breathing and concentration. I think lots of practice with a partner done slowly (just practice and searching. It is the same with them all combined, which will give you mental intent and development.

Is there such a thing as a martial mind – something that is particular to martial practice, or are the mental requirements needed for success in martial arts the same as those needed for success in any physical activity (such as marathon running.

"Yes to them all". Is there such a thing as a martial mind/ "Yes", however the mental requirements to be successful in most things are the same. I know I have done a marathon and I know it takes a lot out of you and you certainly need a strong mind to keep going. The martial mind that I have achieved certainly kept me going. I know I keep coming back to the same answers but it's dedication, determination, hard work and there enjoyment of training, searching and self – motivation.

Doe's successes come from within you? Is it a case of you having it, or you don't? Can the instructor draw success from you?

Doe's successes come within? "Yes" some people have it some people do not. Yes a good instructor can draw success from you; they can give you confidence and enthusiasm to do well.

How important is your instructor/has your instructor been in making you the success you have today?

Very important, I got my enthusiasm from my admiration of my instructors, and have tried to emulate them.

To what do you attribute your present success?

Hard work; and dedication; to myself; to my students; to my teachers;

How important are targets and goals to you? Are grades important/ what they tell you about the holder?

I still have targets and goals, which are to be a good instructor and to continue obtaining good techniques and timing and everything to do with my practice. To be happy in all I do. In addition grades are important, more so in your kyu grades as they do open doors in your practice, as you improve? If the grade in the group is a high standard then it shows in the individual holder, and tells you that, "that person has worked hard".

What are the main physical requirements for success in your art (flexibility, Power, ECT?

Sure you need flexibility and power. If you think of all sports commentators – when they are commentating on sportsmen who start to lose whether it is running, boxing or tennis ECT; he comments and says his legs are gone' for example. It is the same with all practices in Karate or any martial arts if you cannot keep up or fight, ECT; it is your legs that go first, so good strong legs. Leg stretching, low stances will make you strong.

How do you work to develop the physical requirements needed for success?

Hard work! Again low stances and lots of leg stretching. I personally feel better if I am running well. I swim and ride a bike and I do work hard at my sit – ups.

Are there any specific areas of physical training that you feel you have to concentrate on?

Yes on my flexibility to keep my flexibility I have to keep stretching all the time. I could go back very quickly.

How do factors such as age and sex effect training?

Well age effects training. Gene Kelly, a very famous actor and dancer, once said you can never jump as high as when you could, when you were twenty-one.

It takes more effort to get out of the chair as you get older and to keep your fitness, more so after an illness or flu ECT; for me that is hard, particularly as I had Major surgery some time ago. Nevertheless, I am here again and feeling better with my training. As for sex if you mean will it affect my training, the answer is "no", however, if you mean can women train as hard as men then there are no differences.

Are martial arts good for improving your general health?

Yes

How can you improve or develop your technique further?

We can improve our techniques further by searching for new techniques and ideas for ways of utilizing our hips and body, searching for more Yin –Yan of body posture, body posture being very important to all our practices. "Correct distance, timing, and harmony. If your distance is correct and you find your timing then you will find initiative when your opponent's harmony and discord collapses. You then pursue and keep pursuing. If negligent he will recover.

Do you think there are such things as secret ways to make technique more effective?

I don't think there are any secret way, but as long as you are searching for the body movement of a technique then keep practicing it until it becomes your own. Maybe years ago in the old days when I first practiced a teacher may not have told you all there was to know, more so Japanese instructors but mainly from the language barrier.

Do you accept that the X factors exist? X factor is the name given to the disproportional effect of what seemed a relaxed or soft technique, if yes what do you think makes it work?

Yes X factor does exist. This is probably the secret in your last question. However, we in our group it is no secret. A relaxed body and a strong mind with forward focus at all times, even when willing to take a backward step.

To put our ways in words on paper is very hard; however, the only way is to feel a practice the written word can never replace practice. When striking, kicking, or punching the ideal being to pass through rather than hitting the surface of your target.

You never see a boxer making stiff and rigid moves in the ring, as you would see in, say some Karate moves and styles. However, yes. There is a time when the body is firm and strong (focus) but only for a very fleeting moment on contact then it goes' back to being relaxed and soft but firm again.

We find in our group that this is where Tai-chi and Bo practice comes in to help us with our karate, mainly the Cheng Tai-chi

Do you think that the founders of martial arts are very special people? Do you think they have died out now? If no then what does it take to develop a new tradition?

Yes the founders were very special people, but then to become a very good instructor in martial arts, you have to become every special. It takes a lot of time, patience and dedication to become tops at whatever you do in life, whether it is work, Karate or any martial sport.

Let us say that if you wanted to play tennis, then just practicing once a week will mean you will be quite good at it. However, to reach Wimbledon you would have to live with a racket in your hand all the time. Most of our founders in martial arts were brought up on it from an early age.

They have not died, for as long as there are dedicated instructors and martial artist then martial arts and the founders will live forever. New traditions and arts are meliorating all the time. New instructors and dedicated people will always come to the fore.

If you think of founders like Gichin Funikoshi, and going back even further "Monk" Bhodidharma (Daruma) then these people are immortalized forever. Legends like Bruce Lee, Chuck Norris and my own instructors Sensei Mitsusuke Harada, Sensei Vivian Nash, and jimmy Woods.

While there are special people like these founders and their traditions, and new traditions and people from other arts and styles I have not mentioned, but I am only referring to my own origin and history of my karate. I have practiced with other well run organizations one called Bushi there chairman and founder Kevin O'Conner is outstanding on the mat with his martial arts and is very approachable man with a friendly manner.

Going back to what inspired or impressed me about my first instructors; Sensei Vivian Nash was the first sensei that gave me so much. His ability is a testimonial to his impressiveness. He will always remain my father figure in Karate, and the person I will always look up to and refer to in my practice, and to myself, and my students. Thou this does not take anything away from sensei Kevin O'Connor for his operation of techniques are just as effective, but with an open mines to all styles and interpretation of other disciplines. And the sincere recognition for the standard you have achieved in your art; and your teaching ability. At what point does a person interpretation of a tradition become a distinct style in its own right?

Thinking about this, mainly change. Once you bring in changes that style changes. Ok some changes can be for the good. For things do change with time. However, sometimes changes can alter the concepts of technique, which can be a bad thing. Some traditions "must be pursued", at all times, to allow technique to continue to grow.

The word style means that someone trains in this school or that school under this teacher or that teacher. However, to me style means a personal thing to an individual. You can only imitate a person's style, but you will only, "still be you", and not that person. We can train under this person or that person, but style will only be whatever your interpretation of it will be.

How and why does new style come into existence?

Well there are several reasons, some controversial but still true, some good, and some bad. Falling out of instructors, then that person not wanting to train in that style. So they start their own style. Alternatively, someone moves to another part of the country or a person not agreeing with changes in their group ECT. A person may not gain his grades that he/she thinks they deserve. It has been known for a brown belt to leave a group, strap a black/belt around his/her waist, and have people called them Sensei. This does happen. It is a shame but a fact.

How important are titles such as Sifu, Sensei, Sabom and Shihan to you?

Well tae Sifu, and Sensei, they both mean teacher in English, so anybody who is teaching weather it is martial art or writing or a maths teacher is a Sifu or sensei. A Sobon and Sihan being what level teacher you are. To obtain this sort of level takes many years of dedicated practice of training, and if given for the right reason, then these people should be shown the respect they deserve.

Again levels of teaching varies from school to school, and levels of standards. A good teacher or leader is very important and a good atmosphere of respect of traditions will help to produce good clubs.

What does it take to become a Grandmaster?

I do not think any Grandmaster would say they are. His students set him up for it. Any leaders top Sensei's would say I do not deserve this. "A Grandmaster" – where do you go from there? Most teachers would be humbled to this title, but what does it take to be one? Again – everything we have been talking about. Technique, dedication and being a good teacher, (Sifu, Sensei) All and everything.

(Stanislaw once said), -- "to be in vain of rank or place is to show one is below it".

Where do you think martial politics come from?

Marital politics has no right in the DO-Jo. Martial politics usually comes from martial artist that are serious for the welfare of the arts. "Sometimes" good, sometimes bad", can be destructive, usually from school and their differences.

Sometimes – petty jealousies between different styles, which is more successful than the other, in addition, a lot to do with conflicting ideals on rules for competitions ECT;

Trying to be top governing body, this has to do with getting into the Olympics. I have no interest in this (just practice & training).

What would you do to make martial arts more televisable?

I really do not think it will be thorough competitions. I think people have to be educated to know Karate and other martial arts are not just about fighting. Much more can be done for the internal quality's aspects and the grace of movement; "Sequence kata" with sword and Bo, Tai-Chi ECT; and chat shows during and after. "From martial artist", also self-defence.

How would you set about changing public's attitude towards martial practice? What effects do/did the Ninja turtles and the power rangers have on perceptions of Martial arts.

Same as your last question, on discussions, analyzing techniques and Kata, sword, Bo, Tai-Chi in a chat type show on a regular basis. It is not right way with the power rangers, ninja turtles ECT; - but a way.

What ambitions do you have in terms of a (personal' development and development of your association?

To my personal development, that is all I wish is to be able to carry on, to be able to practice. To find more in my technique to carry on my searching to improve in all I do, to be a good teacher and pass on my practice to a new generation.

In addition, our group association can grow with good students going on into life with a good character and development to be a good person.

How do you intend to realize these ambitions?

Just to keep on practicing and keep on communicating.

How long do you think it will take to realize these ambitions?

A life time, "never ending".

What do you need to realize them?

To have a good partner and good health.

Sensei Griffiths Sparring with Dean George in the Gym at Rea Bridge 1980.

Some of the juniors' leg stretching Graham my son on the right

A TEACHERS REPORT
TO BE OBTAINED FOR GRADING WITHIN
THE SHOTO'S TRADITIONAL-KARATE-KAI

To be able to take part in a grading within the Shoto's Traditional-Karate-Kai, we ask you to take this report to your teacher and ask politely, if He/She will not mind filling in the short Questionnaire.

We try to teach a positive and well-mannered attitude, with in the club, and encourage you to do well within school.

Within your /our practice, we expect a student to be on their best conduct and behavior at all times, not just within the boundaries of the Do-Jo, and whilst training. We discourage bad language, racial remarks, sexual remarks or remarks about another child or parent,

Bad manners and misbehaver "will not be tolerated".
This could affect your grades with-in The Shoto's Traditional-Karate-Kai.

We can assure you that by complying with all the rules with-in the grading syllabus, "you will, "and can become" one of our well-respected black belts for the future.

The Sensei, Shihan, and Chief instructor of Shoto's Traditional Karate-Kai
Gerald Glyn Griffiths Esq.

A respected instructor within the management strata of the worldwide organization of Bushi-Karate-Jitsu-Association, (B.K.J.A.). And with the help of his most,
Senior instructor "Robert Huntley Esq.,
Will be able to help you to achieve this.
>>> Good luck and hard work go with you for the future <<<

We solemnly swear to assure you of our best intentions to give you the best instruction possible within the combat arts.
We can be contacted on the Webb site of.
(www.bkjassn.com) or Email to (gjgrif@btinternet.com)

To the teacher.   Student's name-_____ **student:**

How is this student progressing / behaving?

                  Yes   No

(A) Has he/she **tried** to progress in class, to your satisfaction? _____
(B) Do he/she show respect to his/her teachers/elders? _____
(C) Has the student complied with the above practices of? _____
    Shoto's Traditional Karate-Kai? Of his/her behavior.
    That; is expected of him /her within the boundaries of school.

TEACHERS SIGNTURE _____ Stamped if possible

<u>Chief instructor for Shoto's Traditional Karate-Kai.</u>
<u>Shihan Gerald Glyn Griffiths esq.;</u>
<u>Physical activity readiness Questionnaire (par-q)</u>

Name Mr/Mrs/Mis _____ <u>Membership number</u> _____

Date of birth_____ Age

Emergency Contact: _____ Telephone _____-

Doctor or GP: Name _____ Telephone_____

Physical activity is safe for most people. However, some people should check with their Doctor before they start becoming more physically active.
If you are planning to become more physically active than you are now. Start by answering the questions below, if you are aged between 15 and 69 the par-Q will tell you if you should check with your doctor before you start. If you are over 69 years of age, and you are not used to being very active. Check with your doctor.

Please read the questions carefully and answer each one honestly: Check Yes or No.

		Yes	No
(1)	Has your doctor ever said that you have a heart condition and that You should only do physical activity recommended by a doctor.	☐	☐
(2)	Do you feel pain in your chest when you do physical activity?	☐	☐
(3)	In the last mouth, have you had chest pain when you have not being doing Physical activity?	☐	☐
(4)	Do you lose your balance because of dizziness, or do you ever lose consciousness?	☐	☐
(5)	Do you have a bone or joint problem that could be made worse by a change in? Your physical activity?	☐	☐
(6)	Is your doctor currently prescribing drugs? (For example. Water pills) for your Blood pressure or heart condition?	☐	☐
(7)	Do you know of any other reason why you should not do physical activity?	☐	☐

Yes to one or more questions

Talk with your doctor by phone or in person BEFORE you start becoming much more physically active or BEFORE you have a fitness Assessment. Tell your doctor about the PAR-Q and which questions you answered YES. You may be able to do any activity you want – as long as you start slowly and build up gradually. Alternatively, you may need to restrict your activity to one, which are safe for you. Talk with your doctor about the kind of activities you wish to participate in and follow his/her advice. Find out which programmes are safe and helpful to you. ——————————————————————

No to all Questions

If you answered NO honestly to all Par-Q Questions. You can be reasonably sure that you can: start becoming much more physically active- begin slowly and build up gradually. This is the safest and easiest way to go.
Delay becoming much more active:
If you are not feeling well because of a temporary illness such as a cold or a fever – wait until you feel better; or If you are or may be pregnant – talk to your doctor before you start becoming more active.
If your health changes so, you answer yes to any of the above Questions you must tell your consultant to see whether your activity, should be changed
Declaration and Health Waiver.
I have read understood and completed this Questionnaire. Any questions I had were answered to my full satisfaction. I am aware that participation in an exercise programme requires me to be clear of any medical or health problems and any action which I take to engage in a activity is taken with full knowledge of my present and past medical history and waiver the risk of Shoto's Traditional Karate –Kai. I hereby indemnify Shoto's traditional Karate-Kai of any and all activities relating to my use of the club.

Signed _____ Date _____

Chapter (30)   Child protection. The basics

When initiating a new class, always make a set of rules that are cleanly displayed, so that a child knows the boundaries that they are expected to adhere to. Always have a set of sanctions clearly displayed so that a child knows what will happen if the rules are broken.

Where ever possible invite parents to stay and watch the class. Always explain to parents and children, the nature of the martial art, the fact it is a contact sport and the child will be involved in all aspects of the sport.

When you need to assist a child in posture, or need to be hands on in any way, and then explain to the child step by step exactly what you are doing and why you are doing it. As with all martial arts, accidents do happen.

You need to document any accidents no matter how minor you feel it to be, in a comprehensive accident book.

Write yourself a permission slip so parents can sign to give the child permission for the child to take part in the sport and to ensure that they know it is a contact sport and they may get injured.

Where possible, have two or more instructors assisting with the class all the time, this is to assist in control, to witness any incidents that may occur and to assist in teaching. Get to know the children. Trust is a great asset to have with children.

If a punishment is required it is in accordance with what the child is being punished for.

Do not under any circumstances show favouritism to any one child, or particular group of children. Always treat a child from an ethnic minority in the way his race, religion or culture expects. Never make any racial remarks, gender based remarks, Sexual remarks, or remarks about another child or parent, where it may be heard and taken in the wrong content.

In the front right Larrisa Fay Griffiths my Granddaughter. Back row from left Jessica hanks,

Kirstie Cratchley, who became a black belt, which you seen on page 103?
Then Michael Hannis, who I believe went into the armed forces.

Child Protection policy for the protection of Children Within Shoto's traditional Karate Kai

Clear Practices and procedures will ensure that everyone knows and understands exactly, what are expected in relation to the protection of children and young people within our sport and way of life. And participating in Martial Arts, within the Shoto's Traditional Karate Kai. Are able to do so in a safe and enjoyable environment:

It is essential that those children and young people attracted t

In order to protect your children / young people who participates in our Martial arts at our club's: remember it is a contact type of sport. We recognize our responsibility to safeguard the welfare of all children and young people in our care.

If we have to assist a child in posture or need to be hands on in any way then this is explained to the child exactly. Duo to the complexity of the child protection policies lay down.

We do ask parents to be present while the child /young people are training. We also ask that each child, be already changed into their karate suit prior to training.

We show no favouritism to any child or particular groups of children. In addition, all their grading they achieve on purely their own merit they are graded not on just their techniques and ability in Karate but on their behaviour and conduct in all they do. We try to teach a positive and well-mannered attitude, with in the club and encourage doing well within their schooling at school.

There is an accident book. As with all martial Arts, accidents do happen. In addition, no matter how minor an accident it is entered into the book.

Where possible we always have two instructors instructing the class, to witness any incidents that may acure, and to assist in teaching. We also discourage bad language, racial remarks sexual remarks or remarks about another child or parent, where it may be heard and taken in the wrong context.

We the sign parent has given permission for _____

To train at Shoto's traditional karate Kai club.

Have read / filled Questionnaire and sign it _____

Chapter (31)

TAI CHI CHUAN

AS LAID DOWN BY

THE SHOTO'S TRADITIONAL KARATE KAI

Your first lesson
If you have never had a Tai Chi class before

It is important to check your health and fitness. If you have concerns about your general state of health, then talk to a doctor first.

The dress code at our schools is that you should wear loose clothing that will not restrict your movements. At a later date when you know that you will keep training, we wish you to wear our uniform. Bare feet trainers or kung fu slippers to be worn. Generally we warm up with some gentle exercise to prepare the body for the Tai Chi. Warm up will generally take about ten to fifteen minutes.

The types of classes consist of: (1) Tai Chi Basics: This is mainly aimed at the beginners.

Body posture, and Body alignment, Chi gong breathing and energy development.

(2)Tai Chi Forms:

Those that are competent are allowed to practice in groups and explore the Tai Chi forms. For more complexes moves, there is a separate group with instruction at all times, "and for questions". Both classes will have a competent senior grade. Other times there can be one class going at the same time. This way everyone has a chance of every ones experience. There is more time to give demonstrations of technique for all to see from the most senior instructor. Tai Chi Applications: To cover Push hands we need to be in pairs to be able to generate the internal strength, and chin Na and self-defence exercises, and to study the Fajing of the hips.

The Fajing takes its motion mostly from the Chen form. The Chen form is the oldest of the many styles that is practiced today. The characteristics of the Chen being a combination of fast and slow, soft and hard movements.

Page (1)

TAI_CHI SYLLIBUS

(1) (2) (3

(1) WU CHI
(2) TAI-CHI BEGINS WITH BOW
(3) FINDING POSTURE

(4) (5) (6)

(4) GATHER UP BALL
(5) WARD OFF RIGHT
(6) WARD OFF LEFT

(7) (8) (A)

(7) THREE POINT CONCENTRATION

(8A) GRASP THE BIRDS TAIL

(8)(B) (9)

(8B) GRASP BIRDS TAIL PULL BACK

(9) PULL BACK AND PUSH

(10) (11) (A)

(10)   PUSH DOWN AND UP

(11A) DIAGONAL SINGLE WHIP

Page (2) TAI_CHI SYLLIBUS

(11) (B)   (12)   (13)

(14)   (15)   (16)

(17)   (18)   (19)

(20)   (21)   (22)

(23)   (24)   (25)

(26)   (27)   (28)

(11)(B) SINGLE WHIP

(12) STEP UP AND RAISE HANDS

(13) SHOULDER & ELBOW BACK HAND FLICK

(14) THE WHITE CRANE SPREADS ITS WINGS

(15) BRUSH HANDS RIGHT, BRUSH HANDS LEFT

(16) BRUSH KNEE STEP IN PUSH

(17) STEP BACK THREE POINT CONCENTRATION

(18) OLD MAN PLAYS FIDDLE

(19) BRUSH KNEE AND TWIST STEP LEFT

(20) BRUSH KNEE TWIST STEP RIGHT

(21) BRUSH KNEE TWIST STEP LEFT, STEP UP AND PUSH

(22) STEP BACK OLD MAN PLAYS FIDDLE

(23) BRUSH KNEE TWIST STEP LEFT

(24) PULL BACK SCOOP LEFT HALF HAND

(25) STEP UP, WARD OFF AND BACK FIST PUNCH

(26) WARD OFF, PUNCH LOW

(27) APPARENTLY CLOSING UP

(28) CARRY TIGER TO THE MOUNTAIN

Page (3) TAI_CHI SYLLIBUS

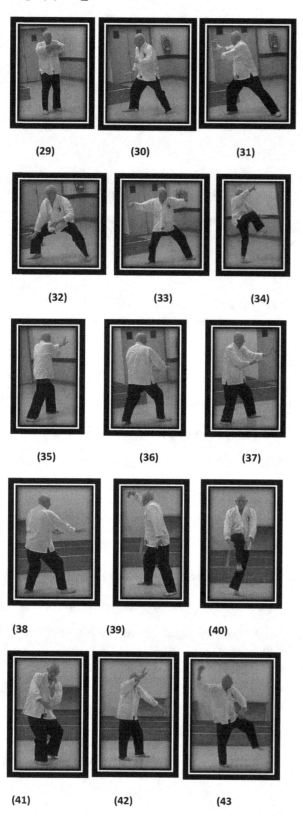

(29)   (30)   (31)

(32)   (33)   (34)

(35)   (36)   (37)

(38   (39)   (40)

(41)   (42)   (43

(29) Cross Hands

(30) Diagonal brush knee twist step left

(31) Three point concentration

(32) Grasp birds tail.

(33) Diagonal Single whip.

(34) Step up Raise hands

(35) Fist under Elbow

(36(Repulse Monkey Left

(37) Repulse Monkey right

(38) Repulse Monkey left

(39) Slanted flying

(40) Step up Raise hands

(41) Shoulder Elbow wrist flick

(42) White Crane Spreads it's Wings.

(43) Brush knee and twist step left

173

Page (4) TAI-CHI SYLLIBUS

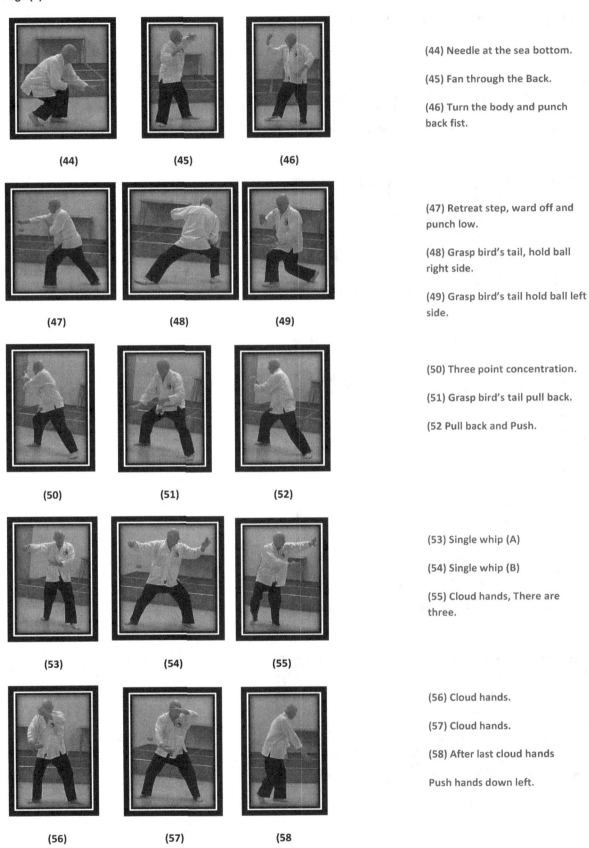

(44) (45) (46)

(47) (48) (49)

(50) (51) (52)

(53) (54) (55)

(56) (57) (58

(44) Needle at the sea bottom.

(45) Fan through the Back.

(46) Turn the body and punch back fist.

(47) Retreat step, ward off and punch low.

(48) Grasp bird's tail, hold ball right side.

(49) Grasp bird's tail hold ball left side.

(50) Three point concentration.

(51) Grasp bird's tail pull back.

(52 Pull back and Push.

(53) Single whip (A)

(54) Single whip (B)

(55) Cloud hands, There are three.

(56) Cloud hands.

(57) Cloud hands.

(58) After last cloud hands

Push hands down left.

Page (5) TAI-CHI SYLLIBUS

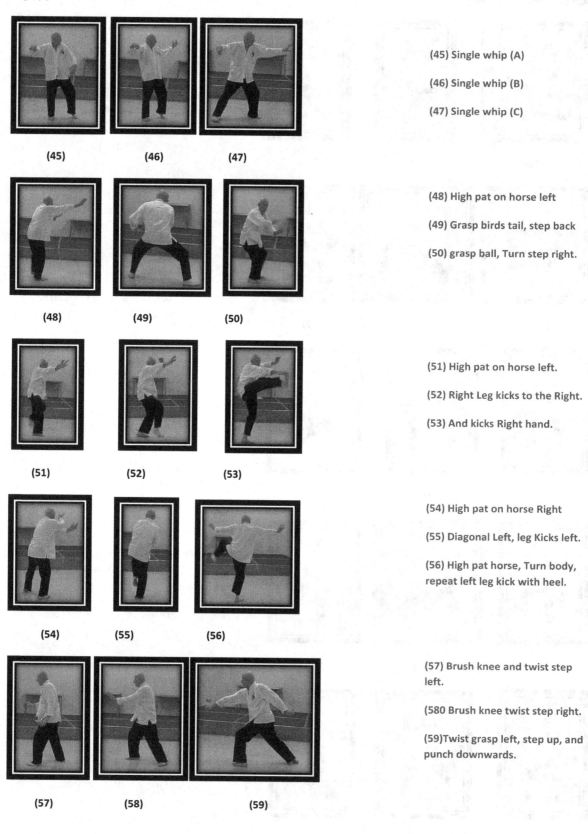

(45) (46) (47)

(48) (49) (50)

(51) (52) (53)

(54) (55) (56)

(57) (58) (59)

(45) Single whip (A)

(46) Single whip (B)

(47) Single whip (C)

(48) High pat on horse left

(49) Grasp birds tail, step back

(50) grasp ball, Turn step right.

(51) High pat on horse left.

(52) Right Leg kicks to the Right.

(53) And kicks Right hand.

(54) High pat on horse Right

(55) Diagonal Left, leg Kicks left.

(56) High pat horse, Turn body, repeat left leg kick with heel.

(57) Brush knee and twist step left.

(580 Brush knee twist step right.

(59)Twist grasp left, step up, and punch downwards.

Page (6) TAI-CHI SYLLIBUS.

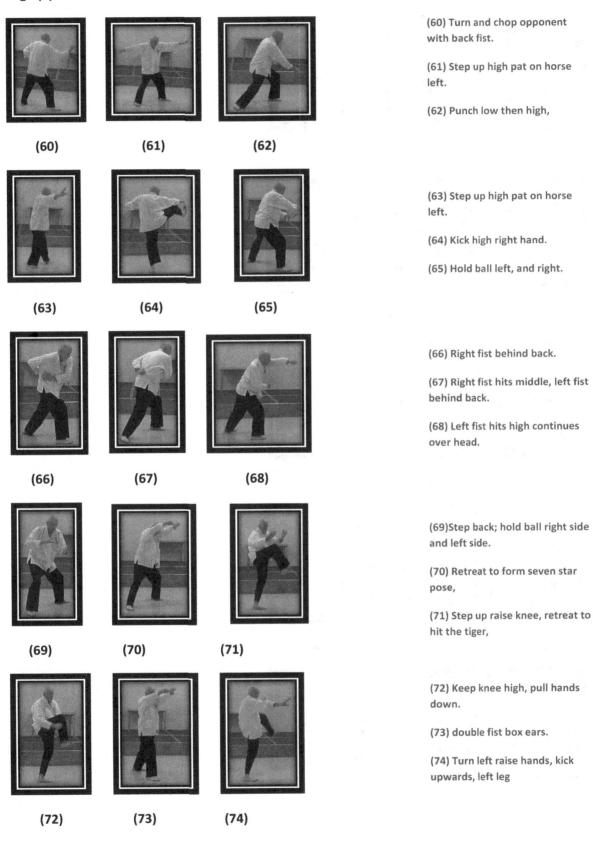

(60) (61) (62)

(63) (64) (65)

(66) (67) (68)

(69) (70) (71)

(72) (73) (74)

(60) Turn and chop opponent with back fist.

(61) Step up high pat on horse left.

(62) Punch low then high,

(63) Step up high pat on horse left.

(64) Kick high right hand.

(65) Hold ball left, and right.

(66) Right fist behind back.

(67) Right fist hits middle, left fist behind back.

(68) Left fist hits high continues over head.

(69) Step back; hold ball right side and left side.

(70) Retreat to form seven star pose,

(71) Step up raise knee, retreat to hit the tiger,

(72) Keep knee high, pull hands down.

(73) double fist box ears.

(74) Turn left raise hands, kick upwards, left leg

Page (7) Tai-chi syllabus, of the Long Yang

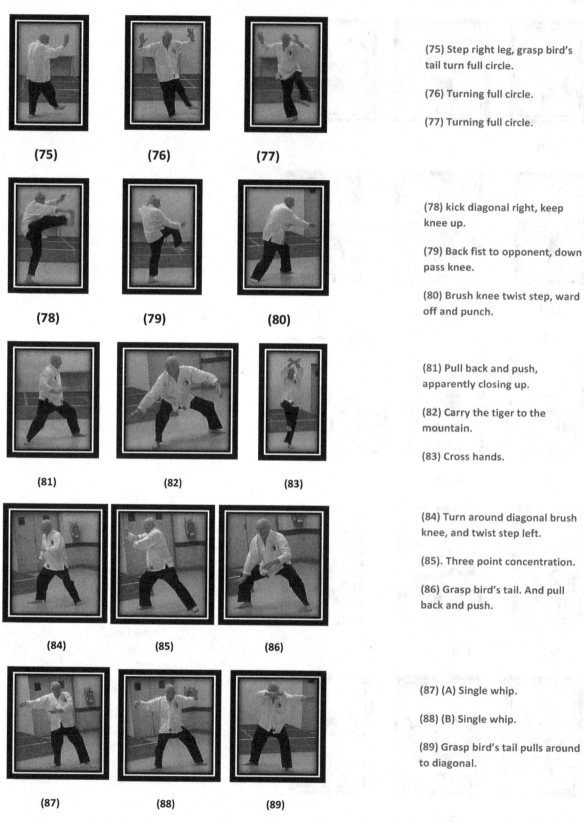

(75) (76) (77)

(78) (79) (80)

(81) (82) (83)

(84) (85) (86)

(87) (88) (89)

(75) Step right leg, grasp bird's tail turn full circle.

(76) Turning full circle.

(77) Turning full circle.

(78) kick diagonal right, keep knee up.

(79) Back fist to opponent, down pass knee.

(80) Brush knee twist step, ward off and punch.

(81) Pull back and push, apparently closing up.

(82) Carry the tiger to the mountain.

(83) Cross hands.

(84) Turn around diagonal brush knee, and twist step left.

(85). Three point concentration.

(86) Grasp bird's tail. And pull back and push.

(87) (A) Single whip.

(88) (B) Single whip.

(89) Grasp bird's tail pulls around to diagonal.

Page (8) Tai-Chi syllabus

(90)   (91)   (92)

(93)   (94)   (95)

(96)   (97)   (98)

(99)   (100)   (101)

(102)   (103)   (104)

(90) Parting of Wild Horse's Mane Right.

(91) Parting of Wild Horse's Mane Left.

(92) Parting of Wild Horse's Mane Right.

(93) Ward off left.

(94) (A) Grasp birds Tail.

(95) (B) from Grasp Birds Tail pull down and back.

(96) Redirect to diagonal left.

(97) Reach out Roll back.

(98) Press and push.

(99) (A) Single Whip.

(100) (B) Single Whip.

(101) Grasp Birds Tail, pull back to Right.

(102) Make energy Ball Right.

(103) Make energy ball, turn over to Left side.

(104) Make energy ball Turn over, to Right side.

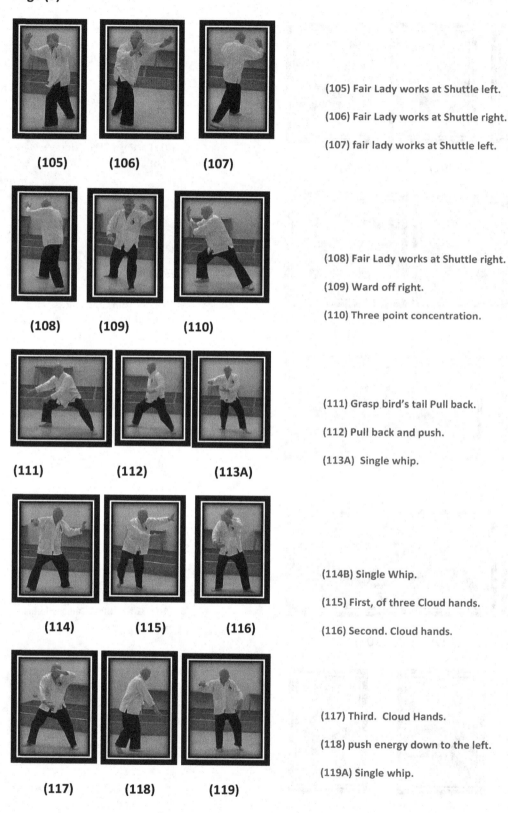

Page (9)

(105) Fair Lady works at Shuttle left.

(106) Fair Lady works at Shuttle right.

(107) fair lady works at Shuttle left.

(108) Fair Lady works at Shuttle right.

(109) Ward off right.

(110) Three point concentration.

(111) Grasp bird's tail Pull back.

(112) Pull back and push.

(113A) Single whip.

(114B) Single Whip.

(115) First, of three Cloud hands.

(116) Second. Cloud hands.

(117) Third. Cloud Hands.

(118) push energy down to the left.

(119A) Single whip.

Page (10)

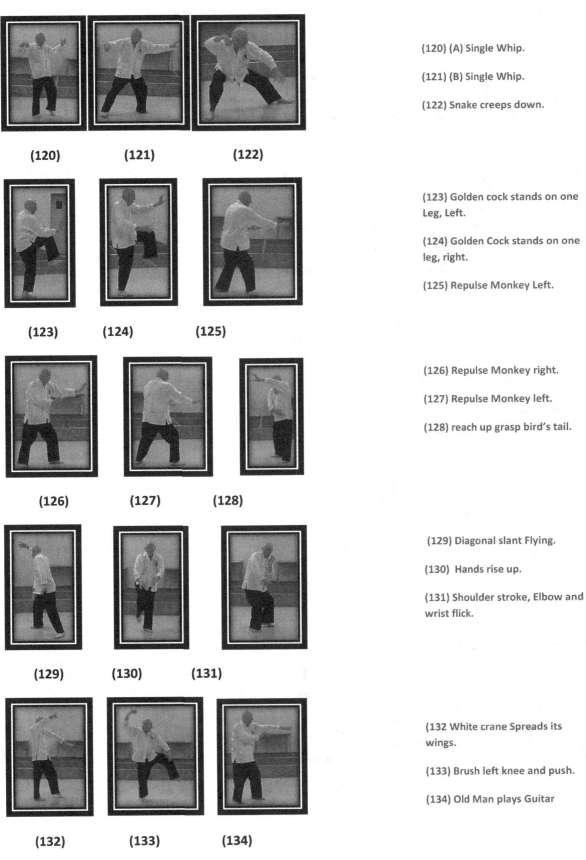

(120)   (121)   (122)

(123)   (124)   (125)

(126)   (127)   (128)

(129)   (130)   (131)

(132)   (133)   (134)

(120) (A) Single Whip.

(121) (B) Single Whip.

(122) Snake creeps down.

(123) Golden cock stands on one Leg, Left.

(124) Golden Cock stands on one leg, right.

(125) Repulse Monkey Left.

(126) Repulse Monkey right.

(127) Repulse Monkey left.

(128) reach up grasp bird's tail.

(129) Diagonal slant Flying.

(130) Hands rise up.

(131) Shoulder stroke, Elbow and wrist flick.

(132 White crane Spreads its wings.

(133) Brush left knee and push.

(134) Old Man plays Guitar

Page (11)

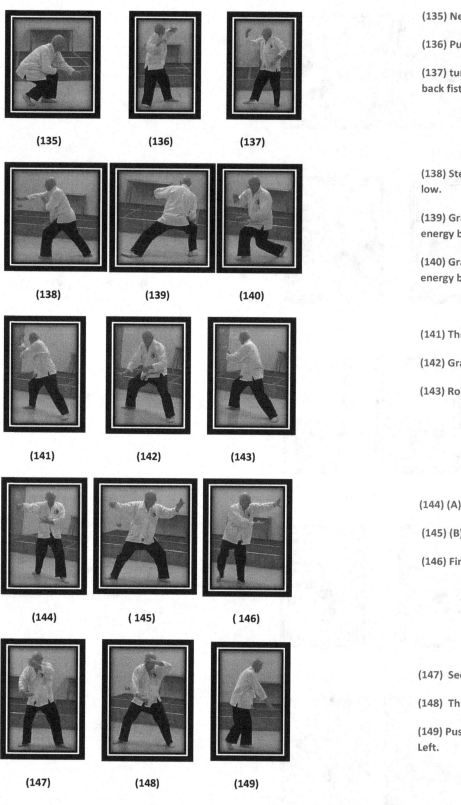

(135)   (136)   (137)

(138)   (139)   (140)

(141)   (142)   (143)

(144)   (145)   (146)

(147)   (148)   (149)

(135) Needles at the sea bottom.

(136) Push through Mountain.

(137) turn block and downward back fist strike.

(138) Step up ward of and puch low.

(139) Grasp birds tail pull down energy ball right.

(140) Grasp birds tail pull down energy ball left.

(141) Three point concentation.

(142) Grasp birds tail pull down.

(143) Roll back and push.

(144) (A) Single Whip.

(145) (B) Single Whip.

(146) First of three Cloud Hands.

(147) Second Cloud Hands.

(148) Third Cloud Hands.

(149) Push energy Down to the Left.

Page (12)

(150) (151) (152)

(153) (154) (155)

(156) (157) (158)

(159) (160) (161)

(162) (163) (164)

(150) (A) Single Whip.

(151) (B) Single Whip.

(152) (C) Single Whip.

(153) Grasp birds tail, Step back,

(154) Strike with side of right hand.

(155) Step in left foot strike with White Snake puts out its tongue.

(156) Intercept deflect.

(157) Open up and kick.

(158) parry Left and right.

(159) Brush Knee twist step left.

(160) Brush Knee twist step right.

(161)Step up ward off and punch to groin.

(162) Grasp birds tail pull back energy ball right.

(163) Grasp birds tail, twist energy ball to left.

(164) Step into three point concentration.

Page (13)

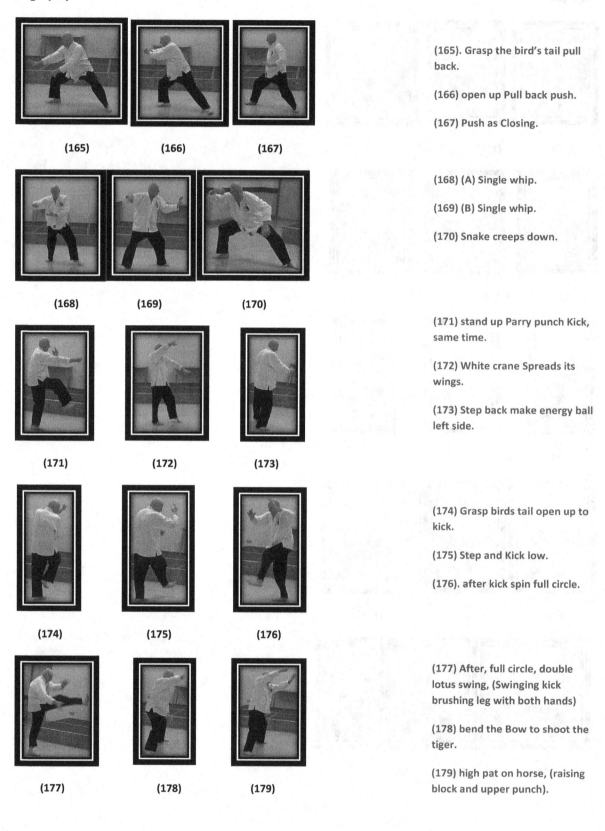

(165)   (166)   (167)

(168)   (169)   (170)

(171)   (172)   (173)

(174)   (175)   (176)

(177)   (178)   (179)

(165). Grasp the bird's tail pull back.

(166) open up Pull back push.

(167) Push as Closing.

(168) (A) Single whip.

(169) (B) Single whip.

(170) Snake creeps down.

(171) stand up Parry punch Kick, same time.

(172) White crane Spreads its wings.

(173) Step back make energy ball left side.

(174) Grasp birds tail open up to kick.

(175) Step and Kick low.

(176). after kick spin full circle.

(177) After, full circle, double lotus swing, (Swinging kick brushing leg with both hands)

(178) bend the Bow to shoot the tiger.

(179) high pat on horse, (raising block and upper punch).

Page (14)

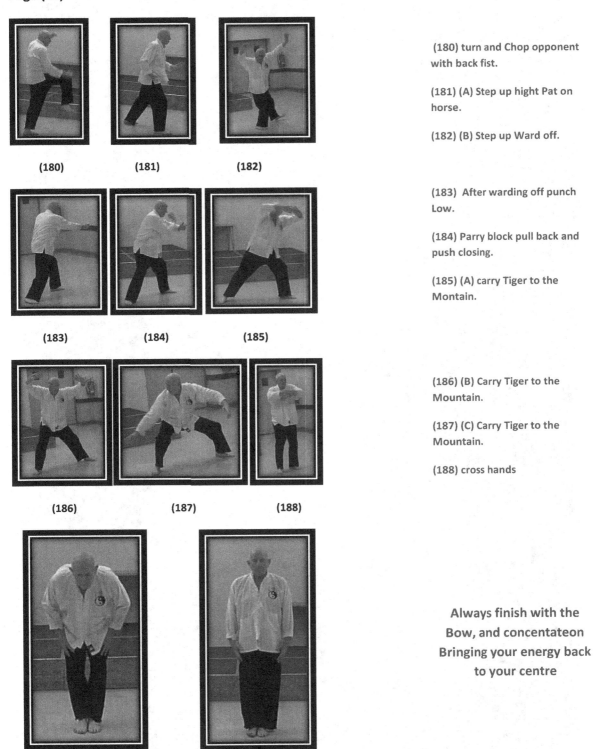

(180) (181) (182)

(183) (184) (185)

(186) (187) (188)

(180) turn and Chop opponent with back fist.

(181) (A) Step up hight Pat on horse.

(182) (B) Step up Ward off.

(183) After warding off punch Low.

(184) Parry block pull back and push closing.

(185) (A) carry Tiger to the Montain.

(186) (B) Carry Tiger to the Mountain.

(187) (C) Carry Tiger to the Mountain.

(188) cross hands

Always finish with the Bow, and concentateon Bringing your energy back to your centre

Chi and the universal energy at the Rea

SYLLABUS
FOR TAI CHI

AS PRACTICED BY

THE SHOTOS TRADITIONAL
KARATE KAI

JUNE MONTROSE GRIFFITHS: 'WARD OFF LEFT'.

Chapter (32)

Tai Chi Weapons.
The Chinese long-staff and broadsword:

For the obvious reasons there is more space needed to practice with the staff because of its length. 'Safety is paramount'. The Long-Staff is used to project your Chi energy, extending beyond the length of the staff. This is during the entire practice of the form.

As well as forms, there are also sparring with pairs. 'Again safety is paramount'. This is practiced with the utmost control, which is the most important part of your grading.

If you can't control your free-style then you can't be trusted to practice.

There are some set practices to be able to help you develop this. There are also some extended ranges of forms to give the practitioner the extending of energy and the turning circle of hips.

Gerald, teaching a Bo Kata at

the Korekushin Ju – Jitsu Association.

The Chinese Broadsword:

Again space is needed, so as to be able to practice safely.

Like the Staff the broadsword is practiced to extend your energy through the weapon, the turning of your hips & the execution of Fajing.

The Chen form:

Within the Chen the Fajing principle is used constantly and it is like a sneeze when the whole body shakes in a jerk like movement.

This movement is joined with the low powerful stances, and the twining coiling movements of explosive releases of power of the fajing. There is shaking shuddering motion of your body as you hit or strike your opponent.

These movements are not so obvious with in the Long-Yang style of Tai Chi.

The long Yang is a constant flow of concentrated energy continuing throughout the entire form Whereas the Chen is fast then slow with these bursts of energies with very low stances.

The grading Syllabus This book is to keep a record of grades.

It is also to give the student some idea of what is expected of "him, her" I. E. dedication to practice, attendance, personal development, E. C. T.
A student will be required to be graded to a physical of proficiency relative to their grade.
Grading will be on the following basis:
Note: the chief instructor at his discretion on any approved association courses can award automatic grading.
Character, Attitude, perfection of stances, basic flowing moves, blocks, strikes, and kicks.

Practice of the forms.

Knowledge and appreciation of techniques. The precision of the form with development of control, speed, power.

Teaching ability and assistance given to others. Searching and understanding of circular movements of the hips, breathing through the Tan Tien (hara).
, Forward and back in posture (ying & yang)
There must be positive mental intent when performing all techniques, with a strong focus of concentration.

Important note:
Members must renew their membership whether grading or not, checks will be carried out on courses.
Club instructors will be responsible for this.

Syllabus Grades to different levels
Stances:
Level (1)
Levels Seven & Six
White & Yellow Sash

Parallel stance:

The horse stance:

These stances will be used for Chi Kung Breathing. The "tan Tien exercise there is a number of these exercises towards developing the internal strength.

The parallel stance:

The sitting stance:

The horse stance:

The treading stance:

The half Split legs:

The single foot stance

All these stances will be practiced moving from one to the other in succession.

The long Yang form
The Long Yang form up to;

The First Carry the tiger to the mountain, and the names of the Tai Chi ch'uan Postures to that level.

Two Man set
You must be able to perform ten moves with a partner of the two man sets.

After this grade you should be able to practice the techniques and exercises you have learnt.

There is no set time to practice but it can be more beneficial in the mornings. Not too much and not too little but don't leave to long between sessions.

Try to keep to a routine. Always warm up before commencing your Tai Chi, avoiding injuries and get the maximum benefits. If you have old injuries that you're trying to heal you have to remember that this training is now therapy practice as well as training.

Sensei, Sifu Gerald Griffiths, Showing what the Tai-Chi movements are for

Level (2)

Levels five & four Orange & Green Level one plus: Push hands 2 Sets.

The Tai Chi forms, up to the second carry Tiger to the mountain, and the names of the postures to that level:

From the first tiger to the mountain and the second tiger to the mountain there are a lot more moves to practice, than from Tai Chi begins, to the first tiger to the mountain.

Which are the first twenty moves of the two-man set:

Level (3) Three & Two Level Blue & Brown Sash Levels 1 & 2 plus the complete Two-man set, "from start to finish".

Complete Long Yang form:

You must know the names of the Tai Chi Ch'uan postures to that level.

Push hands on the move: Free style sticking hands & sensitivity:

Level (4) Level One: Black-Sash Levels (1) (2 (3) plus Complete two-man set both sides:

Complete Long Yang. The names of postures of, tiger to the mountain, "All the way through".

Push hands on the move: Sticking hands free style, "for sensitivity":

The Chinese long staff form: "First form":

So many of the move's of all the discipline's, with my experience 's of mixed training sessions on the mat of Aki-do, ju-jitsu, Ju-do, Karate, and Taekwondo, and kung-fu, I have been able to see most of their techniques in my Tai-Chi.

For years I practiced Tai-Chi without bothering to learn the name of the different techniques, but always looking and studying the application as a martial fighting ability of the technique, rather than the entire fancy name's. It is only now that I have bothered to do so because of writing this book.

By doing so I have been able to give the names of the Tai-Chi technique's to most of say, the Aki-do moves, that I have interpreted it as, "Grasp birds tail" then two "Cloud Hands". Or "Hands plays Guitar", then "Two cloud hands"

The similarities are so clear, if you study and look hard enough at all the many disciplines with all the experiences of different disciplines from mixed training sessions with no blinkers on, then you will discover this yourselves.

The Sensei, Shihan, and chief instructor of Shoto's Traditional Karate Kai Gerald Griffiths Esq. And now represented in Australia Who is a very respected instructor within the management strata of the worldwide organisation of, S.T.K.K.). And with the help of his most senior instructor "Robert Huntley, 5th Dan who is now Chief Instructor of Great Britain.

We can assure you of our best intentions to give the best instructions possible within the combat arts. We can be contacted on the Webb site of

( ) ( )

(Or Email to (

Shihan" Sensei, Sifu

"Gerald Griffiths ESQ"

Sensei" Sifu

"Robert Huntley ESQ"

Gerald holding a pose with a Katana

The Katana is so superb in quality and is a sword worthy of beauty. In Aikido which is by no means the only martial art which uses the Katana; there are others, "Iai-do; Tameshi Giri; and Kendo. Is the art of cutting with the sword? Most of techniques that are taught in the Aikido schools are all linked to the way of the sword. The body and hip movements and postures are all complimentary to sword techniques of the Katana. One of the Weapons we use is the bokken (Ken). The Bokken is a wooden practice sword with similar dimensions and approximate weight, and made of Japanese oak, the same as the katana.

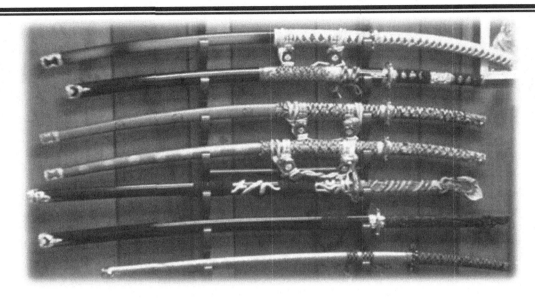

Some of Grandmaster Nenow' Sword's in his DO-JO in America.

The Bokken is now mostly used extensively as a training aid. The movements can be seen as the extension of your hand techniques in say Aikido, and most martial arts, if you look hard enough.

One should always approach training and practice with an attitude of acceptance to the correct instruction of your instructor. Once given your instructions "just practice", if you are at the intermediate beginner's stage, you need to keep your opinions and criticism to yourself, and diligently practice what you have been given; there is no need for talk, Just practice as many repetitions as possible.

The most important thing when practicing with the Bokken (ken) is your posture of your back and look to finding your centre, just the same as finding your centre in all basis for your throwing techniques, and your techniques in karate. By understanding the sword and Bokken techniques you can practice and learn to defend against them. Within Shoto's traditional Karate Kai, we practice with the Bokken quite diligently, practicing to help project our energy, mostly in a spiritual.

The posture and grip of your Bokken is called ("Ken-No-Kamae"). Holding the Bokken must be with a firm but relaxed grip, as shown in the photo lustrated. The both little fingers control the direction of the bokken the angle and projection of your energy. The little finger should be the tightest on your grip; whereas the rest of your hand is being quite relaxed, which allows the shoulders and forearms to be flexible. You need to hold the bokken with your forearms and elbows close to your body and hands a few inches from the body. ("Migi Hanmi") there are seven basic cutting thrust movements

We use a different Bokken to the conventional one; the one we use is a lot heavier, as the one on the right, within Shoto's Traditional Karate Kai; the one on the left is the more conventional one

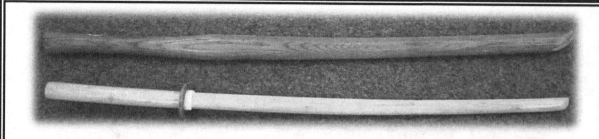

You can see the Bokken's and the difference between the two here

One of the practices in our Karate is to blend with your opponent; Mgi-no-awase, right blending, and Hidari-no-awase, left blending. Tachi dori which roughly in translation means sword taking, the timing for this is so important, if misjudged you will be cut down. A great level of practice and experience is required to reach this senior level and all these practices should be practiced slowly and only build up your speed gradually.

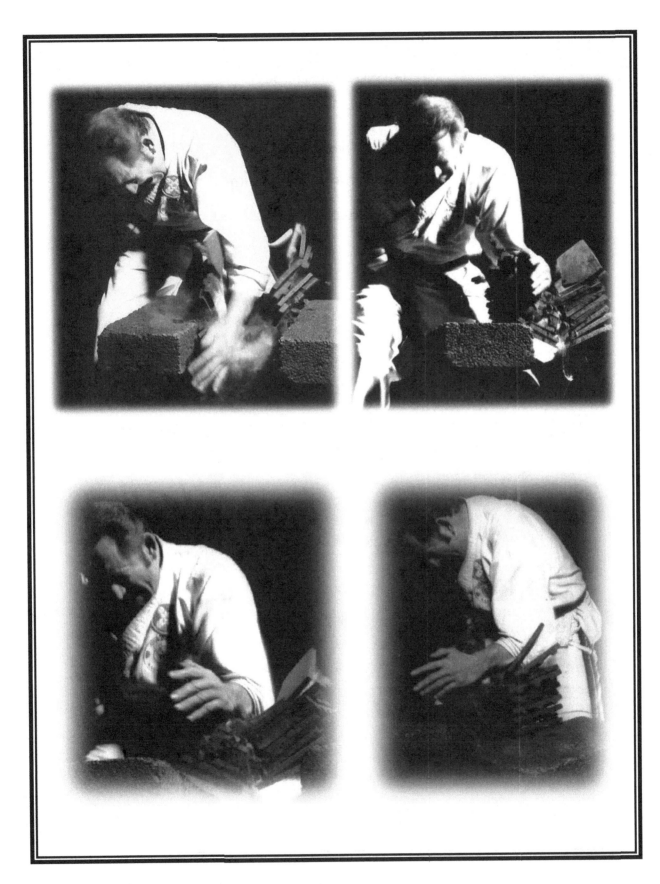

Chapter (33)

JAPANESE TERMINOLOGY

 FOR

SHOTOS TRADITIONAL KARATE KAI

AND FOR MOST JAPANESE MARTIAL ART

Oss	greeting (bow)	
	Yes, I understand	
Seiza	kneel	
Yoi	ready	
Hajime	ready/start	
Yame	stop	
Mawatte	turn	
Mia	front	
Ushiro	back, rear, behind	
Jodadan	aim for the head	
Chudan	aim for the chest	
Gedan	aim below waist	
Mokoso	close eyes	
Mokoso-yame	open eyes	
1	Ichi	
2	Ni	
3	San	
4	Shi	
5	Go	
6	Roku	
7	Shichi	
8	Hachi	
9	Ku	
10	Ju	

Age	rising, upper
Age ate	upper strike, rising Strike
Age tsuki	rising punch
Age uke	rising block
Age ru	to rise, stand up
Ago	jaw
Ago uchi	strike to jaw
Ashi barai	leg sweep
Ashi bo kake uke:	leg hooking block
Ate	strike
Ato uchi	delayed strike (feint)
Awase tsuki	U punch (combined)

Barai oroshi	sweeping drop block
Budo	martial art way
Bunkai	appellation, analysis
Choku tsuki	straight punch
Chudan	middle body
Dachi	stance
Do	way or path
Udo dachi	rooted stance
Fumikomi geri	stamp kick
Ganmen	temple
Gedan	lower body
Gedan barai	lower block or downward sweep
Gedan kakeuke	lower body hooking block
Gedan uke	lower body block
Geri	kick
Gi	karate uniform
Go	hard
Gyaku	from the reverse Position
Gyaku tsuki	reverse punch
Gyaku haito barai:	reverse ridge hand sweep
Gyaku uke	reverse block
Haito	reverse ridge hand
Haito uchi	reverse ridge hand strike
Haishu	backhand
Haishu uchi	backhand strike
Hajime	start or begin
Hasami tsuki	scissor punch
Hayai	fast
Heian shodan	1st kata
Heian nidan	2nd kata
Heian sundan	3rd kata
Heian yondan	4th kata
Heian godan	5th kata
Heiken	flat fist
Heiko uke	parallel block
Heiko tsuki	parallel punch
Heisoku	inside of foot
Heisoku dachi	heals together, attention
Heso	(Tanden) navel
Hidari	left
Hiji	elbow
Hiji uke	elbow block

Kyu	coloured belt rank
Ma ai	distancing
Mae geri	front kick
Mae geri keagi	front snap kick
Mae tobi geri	jumping front kick
Mawashi	round, circular
Mawashi geri	round house kick
Mawashi tsuki	roundhouse punch
Mawashi uke	roundhouse block
Mikazuki geri	crescent kick
mikazuki geri uke:	crescent kick block
Morote	double or two handed
Morote uke	two hand block, 2nd hand braces blocking arm
Morote tsuki uke:	2 handed scooping block
Masubi dachi	informal attention stance heals together toes open 45°
Nage	throw
Nagashi tsuki	flowing punch
Neko ashi dachi:	cat stance
Nihon nukite	2 finger spear hand
Ni dan geri	foot attack from the air
Nukite	spear hand
Obi	belt
Oi geri	lung kick
oi mawashi geri:	round house lung kick
Oi tsuki	lung block
Oni ken	extended knuckle fist
Orei	respect, etiquette
Oroshi	technique coming down from above
Osae uke	pressing block
Oyayubi ippon ken tsuki:	thumb fist punch
Pinan	peaceful mind
Renoji dachi	L stance
Renraku waza	combination technique
Renshu	practice or training period
Sage uchi	drop strike
Sakotsu	collarbone

Barai oroshi	sweeping drop block
Budo	martial art way
Bunkai	appellation, analysis
Choku tsuki	straight punch
Chudan	middle body
Dachi	stance
Do	way or path
Udo dachi	rooted stance
Fumikomi geri	stamp kick
Ganmen	temple
Gedan	lower body
Gedan barai	lower block or downward sweep
Gedan kakeuke	lower body hooking block
Gedan uke	lower body block
Geri	kick
Gi	karate uniform
Go	hard
Gyaku	from the reverse Position
Gyaku tsuki	reverse punch
Gyaku haito barai:	reverse ridge hand sweep
Gyaku uke	reverse block
Haito	reverse ridge hand
Haito uchi	reverse ridge hand strike
Haishu	backhand
Haishu uchi	backhand strike
Hajime	start or begin
Hasami tsuki	scissor punch
Hayai	fast
Heian shodan	1st kata
Heian nidan	2nd kata
Heian sundan	3rd kata
Heian yondan	4th kata
Heian godan	5th kata
Heiken	flat fist
Heiko uke	parallel block
Heiko tsuki	parallel punch
Heisoku	inside of foot
Heisoku dachi	heals together, attention
Heso	(Tanden) navel
Hidari	left
Hiji	elbow
Hiji uke	elbow block

Sakotsu uchi	collarbone strike
sakotsu uchi komi:	collarbone thrusting strike
Sanchine dachi	hourglass stance
Satori	enlightenment
Seiken tsuki	fore fist punch
Shiko dachi	straddle stance(feet turned out)
Shimi waza	strangulation technique
Shita	from above
Shita tsuki	punch to abdomen
Shotei	palm heel
Shotei kekomi	palm heel thrust
shotei oroshi uke:	palm heel drop block
Shotei shita uke:	palm heel block from above
Shotei soto uke:	palm heel block from outside
Shotei ue uke	palm heel block from below
Shotei uke	palm heel block
Shuto	knife hand, sawed hand
shuto ganmen uchi:	knife hand temple strike
Shuto uchi	knife hand strike
Shuto uke	knife hand block
Shuto juji uke	knife hand X block
Shuto kake	knife hand hook
shuto naka uchi	knife hand cross body strike
Shome	front of face
Soku	foot
Sokuto	edge of foot
Sokuto Keage	snap kick with foot edge
Sokuto osae uke	pressing block with foot edge
Soto Uke	outside inward block
Suki	opening
Sukui uke	scooping block
Suwatte	to sit doen
Tameshi wari	test of technique's power
Tate empi uchi	upward elbow strike
Tate shoto uke	vertical knife hand block
Tate zuki	vertical fist punch
Teiji aschi	T stance
Teisho	palm heal
Teisho awase uke	combined palm heel block
Tettsui	hammer fist
Tobi beri	jumping kick
To ho	sword peak hand
Tsrkami uku	grasping block

Tsuki	punch, thrust
Tsumasaki	tips of toes
Uchi	strike, or inside
Uchi uke	inside out block
Ude	forearm or arm
Ude uke	forearm block
Uke	block
Uraken	back fist
Ushiro mawashi geri:	back roundhouse kick
Ushiro mawashi Hiji uchi:	back roundhouse elbow strike
Ushiro moto geri: innerthigh kick	
Yame	stop
Yukuri	slow
Yama tsuki	U punch
Yoko	side
Yoko geri keage	side snap kick
Yoko geri kekomi	side thrust kick
Yoko mawashi enpi uchi:	side round elbow strike
Yoko tobi geri	jumping side kick
Yudansha	black belt holder
Zanshin	awareness
Za zen	seated meditation
Zenkutsu dachi	front stance
Zu tsuki	head thrust

Yoi	Ready
Hajime	Begin! Fight!
Yame!	Stop!
Mawate!	Turn!
Mokuzo!	Concentration/meditation before bowing to partner
Seiza	Kneel!
Sensei-ni rei!	Bow to teacher!
Gedan barai kamaete!	Go into ready stance with gedan barai

Areas of the body

Gedan	Below the belt
Chudan	Between the belt and the neck
Jodan	The head

Kumite	Sparring
Mae	Straight
Makiwara	Striking post
Mawashi	Circular, curved
Migi	Right
Mikazuki geri	Crescent kick
Neko ashi dach	Cat stance
Ren geri	Alternate kicking
Ren zuki	Alternate punching
Shiai	Competition
Tate zuki	Vertical punch
Tsuki	Punch
Uchi	Strike
Uke	Block
Ura zuki	Close punch (short-distance punch without twisting the fist)
Ushiro	Backwards
Yoko	Sideways

Numbers

Ichi	One
Ni	Two
San	Three
Shi	Four
Go	Five
Roku	Six
Shichi	Seven
Hachi	Eight
Ku	Nine
Ju	Ten

Stances

Shizentai	Natural stance
Zenkutsu dachi	Forward stance
Kokutsu dachi	Back stance
Kiba dachi	Straddle stance
Hanmi	Forward stance with hips at 45°
Kamae	Fighting stance
Hungetsu dachi	Half-moon stance (tension towards inside)
Sanchin dachi	Hourglass stance (small stance with tension towards inside)
Sochin dachi	Power stance
	Forward stance, but with back knee open and tension towards outside

Other expressions

Age	Raise
Ashi	Leg
Barai	Sweep
Dojo	Where you train, a club
Empi	Elbow
Fumikomi	Stamping kick
Hara	Physical and mental focus
Hidari	Left
Hiza	Knee
Ippon	One point, once
Jiyu	Free
Kagi zuki	Hook punch
Kakato	Heel
Karateka	Person practising karate
Karategi	Karate suit
Kata	Literally, form: training pattern involving fighting against imaginary opponents
Keage	High snap
Kekomi	Thrust, thrusting movement
Kiai	Karate shout
Kihon	Basic training
Kime	Focus of tension in the body

This is a collage of all the activities in the hall which hung in our Dojo

At

Hardwick village hall in Gloucester England

I sincerely hope you have enjoyed reading about my Life and time's within the

Martial Arts of

Shoto's Traditional Karate Kai.

You can read all about

MY LIFE.

_____And_____

My time in

2nd Battalion Grenadier Guards.

In My Autobiography

Bibliography

31 January at 13:13

Hi'ya,
Vicky I think I did ask you before but I am asking again as I want to be sure. In my book I have done a dedication to Les, would you mind if I put your eulogy in it please? And If you have a good pic of Les throwing someone that would be good, but don't worry I do have some nice pics.
You will like it, there are two books, one is my Biography and life the other one is My Martial arts. Will send a copy soon in PDF.
Kind regards love Griff.

31 January at 15:07

That would be fine Griff I will sort out the Eulogy and a photo for you xx.